Pathways and Passages to
Leadership

DAVID J. SMITH

AuthorHouse™
1663 Liberty Drive
Bloomington, IN 47403
www.authorhouse.com
Phone: 1 (800) 839-8640

Published by AuthorHouse 4/29/2016

ISBN: 978-1-5246-0172-0 (sc)
978-1-5246-0173-7 (e)

Library of Congress Control Number: 2016905433

Print information available on the last page.

authorHOUSE®

PATHWAYS AND PASSAGES…

…To Leadership

A collection of lessons dedicated to those willing to dream the impossible while seeking the improbable.

Inspirational thoughts to help identify the passages that lead from where you are to where you wish to be – that give hope to those having lost their way along life's journey to success.

PATHWAYS AND PASSAGES…

A collection of lessons dedicated to those willing to dream the impossible while seeking the improbable…

> *To those willing to reach for the stars when establishing their reality…*

> > *To those who would accept what could be as a destination rather than being content to live life within what is…*

> *To those willing to innovate as they fulfill their dreams…*

To those accepting the responsibility for INDIVIDUAL ACCOMPLISHMENT within a world that too often rewards the accomplishments of society…

> *To those accepting the responsibility of INITIATING CHANGE within a world that too often rewards stability and the status quo…*

> > *To those accepting the responsibilities of LEADERSHIP within a world that too often shifts blame and seeks credit…*

> *To those accepting the responsibilities of LIFE within a world that too often rewards the way things are (or have been) rather than what they could be "if only…"*

A book of thoughts to help identify the passages that lead from here to there – that give hope to those having lost their way during the journey…that provides support to those in need.

A TRAVELLER'S GUIDE TO PATHWAYS AND PASSAGES TO LEADERSHIP...

PATHWAYS AND PASSAGES TO ACHIEVEMENT...

- We Can Achieve All That We Believe If We Believe That We Can Achieve
- Think BIG If You Wish To Achieve
- Do You Have A Personal Mission Statement
- All Things Are Revealed To Those Who Seek (AND Provided To Those Who Act)
- Where You Live Determines How You Live
- Establish The Future By Realizing Your Potential To Define Your Reality
- Share Your Life – Realize Your Dreams
- Intentional Actions Move Us From What Is Probable To What is Possible
- Let Go Of The Past But Hold On To Your Dreams

PATHWAYS AND PASSAGES THROUGH CHANGE...

- When Should We Look For (And To) Change
- Influencing And Motivating Others To Succeed
- Embracing Change
- Much Can Be Accomplished Without Running Away
- Moving Forward Requires Letting Go
- Resolving To Change
- Creating (Or Allowing) Behavioral Change
- Turn! Turn! Turn! – All Change Begins With An End
- Implementing Change
- Transformational Wisdom – Intentionally Applying Knowledge In Pursuit Of Truth

<u>PATHWAYS AND PASSAGES TO ACHIEVEMENT…</u>

A collection of lessons dedicated to those willing to dream the impossible while seeking the improbable…
To those willing to reach for the stars when establishing their reality…
To those who would accept what could be as a destination rather than being content with what is…
To those willing to innovate as they fulfill their dreams…
To those accepting the responsibility of INDIVIDUAL ACCOMPLISHMENT within a world that too often rewards the accomplishments of society.

WE CAN ACHIEVE ALL THAT WE BELIEVE IF
WE BELIEVE THAT WE CAN ACHIEVE

We often receive an unexpected boost from motivational quotes. Many originate within the world of sports BUT life is more than playing games – it is about dreaming what might be our reality if only that which is could become what we hope, wish and dream it to be. It is about reaching beyond our wildest expectations to grasp a slice of reality from a pie not yet baked. It is about setting goals beyond what is achievable so that we force ourselves outside of the box in which we are comfortable and move towards things yet to be considered by standing upon the cardboard to search for those things that have not yet been imagined. We all stumble and fall while travelling through life – the difference between success and failure being whether we stay down or we get back up – and what we learn from the experience.

People react to challenges differently. Some seek comfort from every storm – preferring to remain within the safe harbors of life, never venturing outside the protected coastal waters as they accept the remnants and wreckage that wash up to shore. They allow others to seek new adventures – to conquer unknown territories and discover treasures far beyond their ability to imagine. They are gulls finding sustenance in things discovered and discarded by others. To them, a gentle breeze may appear to be a raging storm – the tranquility of their calm disrupted by even the smallest pebble tossed into the sea. If one were to equate such an existence to the hyena it would be apparent that scavengers ARE able to exist. Rarely, however, does an individual reach greatness when they rely upon "pack mentality" to survive NOR does one receive the "first fruits" when they gratefully accept what comes to them rather than seeking to discover how much more might be available if only they were to stretch beyond their accepted paradigm.

Others seek adventure – preferring to march into the storms of life head on and face forward. They hear the howling in the wind and seek to identify its source – wish to find where it came from before watching it go away. They recognize that the wind cannot be contained nor captured but often dream of riding upon it – of soaring above the earth that holds them as they seek new horizons not yet discovered. They prefer to identify opportunities as they move boldly forward in life rather than seeking comfort in what they (or someone else) already accomplished. Where some could not fathom being a hawk hurtling down towards an unknowing prey, these individualists could not tolerate being a scavenger relying upon the efforts of another for sustenance. Their need for autonomy – for independence – is far too great to accept the path forged by others. They capture the wind within billowing sails – riding it as far as it may take them without allowing their concern for a safe return to detract from the journey. They accept potential peril as the inevitable return on their unrestrained investments towards the accomplishment of their dreams.

As we move through life we must leave our yesterdays behind as we pass through our today in anticipation of all that tomorrow might bring. Unless we fill our emotional pantries with thoughts and visions of grandeur – with hopes and promises of a yet to be defined future reality rather than doing as we have always done while expecting different things to happen to us – we MAY find momentary happiness but will never find the peace to accept that "what is" is all that "could be." Whenever you begin to feel that "where you are" is better (rather than just safer or more secure) than "where you could be," consider the following:

- **As you begin (or refresh) your journey through life, take time for the little things to become big.** Do not move so fast that you fail to enjoy the journey as you seek a destination BUT do not become so enamored with the journey that you never rest or recharge along the way. Find time to help others along the way – to share your strengths and experiences so they might be built up rather than run over. When the going gets tough others may be the only lifeline available to keep us going.

- **Live life to its fullest – focusing as much on the joy in the journey as you do the gold at the end of the rainbow.** More than anything, find peace and joy in all that you say and do – seeking comfort from your discoveries rather than being satisfied to discover comfort within the status quo. Seek moments of rest as you seek to fulfill your dreams rather than sanctuaries and safe havens that might keep you from reaching beyond the shelter of today to experience the potential of tomorrow.

Some find that motivating thoughts or inspirational phrases keep them moving forward rather than looking back. In order to experience gain within our lives, we must realize change – and must keep our eyes on the prize as we move relentlessly towards it if we expect to grow. Thankfully, all thoughts ARE NOT sports metaphors - some of the thoughts I find most helpful including:

- *Dreams take time, patience, sustained effort, and a willingness to fail if they are ever to become anything more than dreams – Brian Linkoski*

- *The greater danger for most is NOT that our aim is too high and we miss, but that it is too low and we reach it - Michelangelo*

- *We know what we are, but know not what we may be - Shakespeare*

- *When the winds of change blow, some people build walls while others build windmills - Chinese proverb*

- *If all you seek to become can be defined by what you have accomplished, accept comfort in who you are but allow those who know you mourn the death of what you may have become.*

There is no limit to what we can accomplish when we seek results and conclusions rather than recognition and credit. We can find ongoing satisfaction when we claim success during the journey – acknowledging each step taken as we run the race rather than waiting until our quest has ended to find satisfaction in the efforts we exhibited. We gain much from life when each step is celebrated as an accomplishment rather than looking only to the goal at the end of our journey as a win/lose, make it or break it destination.

We cannot allow our eyes to drift from the prize if we seek to move from "good" to "great" in our lives. Though it may not "take a village" to raise our self-awareness, it DOES take commitment, determination and intentional action to move beyond the storms that often darken our lives to the pot of gold at the end of a rainbow. Accept nothing but your best as you seek new destinations – learning from your failings as you turn adversity into opportunity while reaching new heights with each passing day. Capture the wind to move forward after each accomplishment rather than finding comfort and accepting as final the rest stops along the way and each never ending beginning will lead towards the better life you wish for.

THINK BIG IF YOU WISH TO SUCCEED...

Change, like life, happens with or without any help from us. Growth, however, comes only through our intentional actions. People love and hate change at the same time. While wishing for things to remain the same in our lives (comfort, security, job, environment, friends, relationships), we really want them to get better (rarely wanting discomfort, negative change or inconvenience in our lives). Wanting it "both ways," we often refuse to invest the necessary "sweat equity" to make change happen. When handed to us, we are more than happy to take it. We are less likely to actively identify areas needing change then intentionally acting to put them behind us while moving forward in a different direction – leaving behind what is comfortable (and holding us back) while hoisting our sails to capture the winds of a new tomorrow (venturing into unknown territory holding not yet realized opportunity). Though we may not always know where the winds will lead us, simply catching hold of their endless power will help us to move from our current reality to a future possibility without becoming caught in the calm between what was and what could be.

Some random thoughts to help maintain focus along the journey from what we know to what we might only imagine – from what is to what could be – would include:

- ***The only way of finding the limits of the possible is by going beyond them into the impossible (Arthur C. Clarke).*** When we restrict our actions, reactions and responses to the ways and methods we have always used, nothing will change. Only when we dare to act in ways we have never before acted – to think in ways we have never before thought – will those things that were once beyond our reach become possible. In order to maximize the likelihood we will succeed, however, we must acknowledge the resistance we will face, respond to the concerns our detractors will present, and present a plausible, acceptable alternative (which is more desirable, beneficial or providing of more opportunity) than the status quo. To move from where you are to where you wish to be, and perhaps even beyond to where you have not yet imagined, tear down the walls that limit you to what you have always known or you will end up doing what you have always done and being what you have always been.

- ***Nothing will ever be attempted if all possible objections must first be overcome. (Samuel Johnson).*** Allowing an individual to learn from failure is possibly one of the best learning techniques we can use. When a person must turn back due to unexpected rapids after charting a course and setting sail, two things happen. First, the individual will (hopefully) learn from his or her mistake by recognizing the signs of turmoil and acting to avoid them before venturing into the unknown again (recognizing the need to continue as being the critical component of learning). Secondly, though, and perhaps more important, we must identify the reason success was delayed and correct the error, mistake or poor judgment in a way that allows us to overcome the obstacles that kept us from progressing towards the accomplishment of our goal. Learning by experience is much more beneficial than listening to someone else say which way to go or what road to take. We should plan, anticipate and think of reasonable alternative approaches prior to starting any task BUT avoid "analysis paralysis" (refusing to move forward if there is ANY chance that something might go wrong allowing our fear of failure to diminish our chances of success). When we never leave the blocks we cannot compete and it becomes impossible to finish the race.

- ***The only person who never makes mistakes is the person who never does anything (Denis Waitley).*** Life is not a carefree path we take while moving towards an idyllic destination. Life is fraught with pitfalls, traps, snares and impossibly steep embankments. It would be nearly impossible to go through life without making a mistake so quit trying to be perfect! Some of the world's greatest inventions have been the unexpected outcomes from failed experiments. Our greatest presidents frequently tasted defeat before they were elected. Many business owners have failed in an endeavor before experiencing success. Once a path has been taken that leads to a dead end – a process selected that results in set-back – learn from it so your next steps can be successful.

- ***Knowing is not enough; we must apply. Willing is not enough; we must do (Johann Wolfgang von Goethe).*** Value is established not by what we know but rather by how we can apply it. Wisdom is the result of applied knowledge. Knowing that a car needs an engine, a transmission, an electrical system and a variety of other mechanical parts does not make you a mechanic. You must apply what you know to be of any use to anyone. I could THINK about fixing a car all day long but nothing would happen until I pick up a wrench (then without proper education, training and knowledge my efforts might cause more harm than good). Any action creates an opposite and equal reaction, both in physics and in life. Intentional action is a prerequisite to change. Plausible and acceptable actions – often outside the normal realm of reasonable and expected responses – are the precursor of success.

- ***Risk more than others think is safe. Care more than others think is wise. Dream more than others think is practical. Expect more than others think is possible (Cadet Maxim).*** As you dive headlong into life, remember that you will get from life only what you put into it. I have seen individuals slide through life expecting (and receiving) very little. Some say they set low goals so they will not fail – that when the "bar is low," nothing will keep them from crossing it. I choose a different path – and so should you. Take calculated risks in order to increase your chances of success. Choose to care more about others than you care about yourself. You might be surprised how rich and free your life will be in return. Choose to dream enough so that you can experience new horizons when bringing dreams to fruition. You cannot fulfill another's dream (no matter how hard you might try), only your own. As for expectations – you will never rise higher than you expect yourself to rise, nor fall lower than you allow yourself to fall.

- ***Focus more upon "what has yet to be done" than "what has been completed" when seeking change. Acknowledging and recognizing your weaknesses helps identify the causes of problems – developing and leveraging your strengths produces long-term solutions (Dave Smith).*** Do not focus upon what cannot be done – continually stretch to achieve those things that have not yet been attempted, reach outcomes that have not been previously accomplished, or choose paths that nobody has yet dared to travel. Do not seek an escape from reality – embrace the potential around you. Do not dwell upon what has been done – seek what has yet to be realized. Always expect more than may seem possible – refusing to accept anything previously accomplished as anything more than a resting point as you seek yet to be discovered destinations – and you will surely taste success!

DO YOU HAVE A PERSONAL MISSION STATEMENT?

Every organization must have a mission – a vision – a reason for "being." Unless an organization exists to fulfill a specific (and necessary) purpose – to produce a product or provide a service – it will not survive. Unless consumers or a market segment needs a product or service (it has, creates or enhances value), the best or largest "supply" in the world will not be "in demand" enough to justify its ongoing presence. Though a business can (and does) impact society by providing jobs, work is a necessary part of the process of producing results NOT the result of an organization's efforts to create meaningful activity. Work without purpose may keep an organization busy (for a time) but will not produce the income needed to sustain its activities. An organization will not be able to attract and retain employees unless it can clearly and definitively communicate what kind of work is expected to be done, how "success" will be measured and how results will be rewarded. Without a mission, an organization cannot focus its resources towards the accomplishment of an identified purpose, choose the direction it should go or qualify the decisions it must make as it establishes itself as being a vital and contributing part of the business community.

In order to be effective, an organization's mission statement must clearly (and concisely) define why a business exists, what it does, and (sometimes) who it serves in a way that can be easily remembered and communicated by all involved in its accomplishment. Nike has established the phrase, *"To bring inspiration and innovation to every athlete in the world"* as its mission statement – implying what it does by who it serves. *«Our mission: to inspire and nurture the human spirit one person, one cup and one neighborhood at a time»* is the stated purpose of Starbucks Company, never mentioning coffee but referring to the inspirational experience it hopes to provide. Coca Cola's mission, *"To refresh the world - in mind, body and spirit; To inspire moments of optimism - through our brands and actions; To create value and make a difference everywhere we engage"* states what the company does without ever saying what it produces. Kohl's mission, *"To be the leading family-focused, value-oriented, specialty department store offering quality exclusive and national brand merchandise to the customer in an environment that is convenient, friendly and exciting"* says what it is without limiting itself to any one particular product or brand. The Employers' Association's mission is *"To provide practical Human Resource solutions to West Michigan business promoting operational excellence and sustainability,"* defining what we provide, to whom it is provided and what our service is intended to accomplish. While no two mission statements are the same, each successful enterprise must be able to state why it exists by communicating what product, service or value is being provided in a way that people understand – and can hopefully easily remember when a need materializes.

Individuals often accept that business needs a mission – a purpose and reason to exist – but fail to transfer that essential reality to their own lives. In order to establish value in ourselves, everyone needs to establish a PERSONAL mission statement to guide individual actions, efforts and activities. A personal mission statement is a bit different from a company mission statement, but the fundamental principles are the same – it provides clarity and a sense of purpose. It defines who you are and how you will live. When we drift without purpose towards an unidentified objective, we will take a long time to accomplish nothing. While we cannot miss a target unless it has been clearly identified and posted – cannot fail unless we establish goals and objectives – life without purpose becomes meaningless. A sailboat needs a sail (to capture the wind) and a rudder (to set a course) if it is to move forward. It needs a keel to stabilize its journey and an anchor to hold it in place during times of rest. Though there are many parts and pieces that work together to make a sailboat move ahead, unless a destination has been identified and deliberate action is taken to move towards it, the best wind, the most favorable seas and the mildest conditions will be wasted unless a "reason to sail" has been established. Unless we (personally) know what we wish to accomplish through the actions we take and the decisions we make, we will never learn what we need to know (do or understand) in order to add value (to ourselves, our friends or our society) as we seek to make a difference in this life. We must dedicate our actions, our efforts and our thoughts towards the accomplishment of SOMETHING if we hope to accomplish ANYTHING.

Writing a personal mission statement offers the opportunity to establish what is important, often allowing us to make a decision to stick to it before we waste energy and resources without knowing where we might want to go. As we establish a personal mission statement, we should seek to ask the right questions rather than trying to provide the correct answers – to expand our horizons to regions we have not yet explored rather than limiting them to our "known and comfortable" universe. An individual mission may be as simple as *"I will make a difference in all I say or do,"* or *"I will live everyday with Integrity and vow to make a positive difference in the lives of others utilizing my knowledge for the good of all people."* It may a "short term" objective like, *"I will complete my education so that I can pursue a new career."* It may be as complex (and convoluted) as, *"I will pursue knowledge that can, through intentional actions and experiences, be transformed to wisdom. I will apply wisdom to advance myself (and others around me) while seeking and establishing new opportunities that add value to my life and my community. I will never give up (though I may occasionally give in) while realizing all that I might hope or imagine myself to be."* Make your dreams become reality by "memorializing" them in writing – by telling another about them so they can hold you accountable for their fulfillment. However you wish to establish a personal mission statement, consider Steven Covey's reference in **First Things First** – that it must connect your own unique purpose with the profound satisfaction that comes from fulfilling it. Life fulfilled is life worth living!

ALL THINGS ARE REVEALED TO THOSE WHO SEEK AND PROVIDED TO THOSE WHO ACT

Those who continually seek that which they do not have – who reach for the stars without knowing whether it is night or day – who always seem to want what others have because they feel their own gifts or abilities are somehow inferior – will probably always be lacking in some way or another. They will never "arrive" as they are always "seeking to go" in a different direction. They are like seeds drifting upon the winds – moving from one place to another without ever taking root so that they might grow. They may enjoy many starts and stops in life – travelling upon a multitude of roads yet experiencing much frustration for they seldom remain on one path long enough to find its conclusion. Rather than living their own life and experiencing the richness it might bring they seek those things others have accomplished as they skim their enjoyment from the surface of life's ocean – plucking only the floating debris left behind rather than diving deeply to find treasures not yet discovered.

Those who feel they have all they could ever need – who do not desire any reward beyond what they have achieved – who always find comfort in "what is" rather than being the least bit curious about "what could be" – will probably find contentment in their life but may never realize their full potential. People finding happiness in the "here and now" without ever seeking to expand their horizons often live lives that are "safe" yet uneventful. They find that travelling a familiar path to a known destination provides a predictable life – an outcome that may not excite but that will never disappoint. They seek to avoid disillusionment by holding tightly to predictability – to eliminate defeat by seeking only that which will provide ongoing rewards (regardless of how large or small the reward might be). Though many find comfort within the familiar walls of a predictable reality, few find the joy of discovery. Though many find contentment within a predictable world, few find their dreams fulfilled or their future altered drastically when they seek shelter from life's storms within their established safe harbor – when they forfeit any thought of the possible for a deeply rooted belief in the here and now.

The secret to being all that you can be – to balancing your abilities against your capabilities while blending the comfort of where you are with the promise of what you might wish to achieve – is in setting realistic goals that stretch your reality from what is to what has not yet been accomplished. Intentional action must be initiated if change is desired – for to see or experience new things one must physically, emotionally or perceptually alter their current situation so the confining walls of "what is" can be broken down and exchanged for the limitless sea of "what could be." While one may never fail if goals are not established, how can one measure progress unless an objective – or destination – has been determined? How can one move forward if they do not know when to stop – or even when to start – doing something different? While one rarely tastes defeat when they choose to live within their familiar world, they cannot savor those things not previously considered possible until they decide to do act differently rather than simply expecting altered results without changing their predictable behavior.

Life is not a spectator sport – it is an interactive opportunity to transform the present into the future (but does not do so on its own). It provides us with the canvas upon which dreams may become reality (but we must act if we are to create such a masterpiece for it will not materialize on its own). Knowing the right answers to questions asked by another might help us overcome obstacles that could hinder our progress as we seek to accomplish defined things. Leveraging our knowledge and experience to ask the right questions is much like planting seeds – if nurtured and cared for, our ideas will be brought to fruition. When we act upon the information we receive from the questions we ask our dreams will become seeds ready for harvest. Recognize, though, that as much as it might wish to become an apple tree, a cherry pit will not grow into anything other than a cherry tree. In the same manner, our ideas and dreams must be plausible – we must have the knowledge, skill and ability to act once a path to success has been identified – if we are to enjoy the things found through our seeking, receive the benefits of our asking and achieve the rewards of accomplishing the goals we intentionally and deliberately set.

WHERE YOU LIVE DETERMINES HOW YOU LIVE

Some live in the past – holding on to the accomplishments of the past far too long. They value tradition (often to the point that they will not venture from the past into the present). They may have pictures of old teams and outdated certificates on the wall – living within their memories – holding on to days gone by as if they were still the most important times of their life. These people find comfort in knowing "what was" rather than thinking about "what could have been" or "what might yet be." People living within their past often hold on to "the old ways" because they worked – never imagining they may not continue to work in a changing world. "Fiddler on the Roof" was a movie about these individuals. Strong, value-driven and steeped in tradition, the culture of the times often held onto tradition to guide their daily lives – but the family depicted found that letting go of the past was an essential part of moving into a modern era. Individuals holding onto "what was" as they live "what is" often seek obstacles that might prevent them from changing rather than actively seeking opportunities that might lead them to things not yet realized.

Most individuals live in the present – finding both satisfaction and a belief that they are achieving their fullest potential by fulfilling their routines and daily activities. They rush from one task to the next without questioning why, knowing only that one thing must be done before moving on. These "present dwellers" are firefighters. They see a problem, throw themselves fully and totally into its resolution, and then move on to the next issue. They are always on the move, often frustrated (and seemingly frenetic), frequently too busy to enjoy the beauty around them. They often appear to travel well beyond the speed of light – buzzing through anything unfortunate enough to be in their paths – moving erratically towards what they are convinced is a well-defined destination. While these people are valuable "doers," they may be unable to enjoy the fruits of their labor because "so much needs to be done in so little time," usually running out of month before their projects are done and losing sight of "the big picture" as they rush to accomplish the "means" without thinking about the "ends." They may find themselves too busy "doing for today" to ever "dream of tomorrow."

A precious few live within the world of "what could be…if only." They do not limit themselves to "what must be done" for they would prefer to dwell within the realm of "why not try doing it differently?" Rather than accepting that tasks and objectives must be accomplished in a prescribed order they live in a world that questions the reason behind every action they take. While they consider the past, they refuse to dwell within it – or to limit their possibilities to the realities of others. Rather than perfecting "what is", they prefer to do what must be done to build towards what has not yet been fully formulated. You can recognize these individuals by their passion – by their outward expression of the attitude that nothing is ever quite good enough because it can always be improved. They cannot seem to stop themselves from saying things like "… that is really good, but have you thought about…" or "That is a great start…" when you present a solution for their consideration. Accepting "what is" as a destination is not an option as they prefer to linger just long enough within "today" to gather the resources necessary for them to spring towards the next opportunity. The movie "Field of Dreams" would depict this world. Considered by many to be dreamers who not only fail to act responsibly but also fail to recognize reality – these individuals truly believe that if they build a dream, something will come of it (and if they accept the status quo, nothing will ever change).

Where do you live in this world? Do you live in the past – anchored within the tradition that has guided people to security for years? Do you live in the present – seeking to accomplish life's daily tasks and challenges? Do you live for a yet to be identified future – seeking progress today so that you can move into tomorrow? Not everyone can be a futurist (nor can we all be historians or content to accomplish daily tasks). We do, however, need components of all these characteristics – people dwelling within the past, the present, and the future – to have a winning team. It is important that we identify "where we live," however, then embrace it as move forward. In order to contribute to a thriving organization one must recognize and acknowledge his or her strengths (values and beliefs) and add to the overall good of their community. When we recognize and embrace individual uniqueness – actively making it a vital part of each relationship (whether at work or at home) we begin to define what could be rather than focusing upon what is (or has been). Only when one is able to move past yesterday's history, beyond the (far too often) mundane realities of today while seeking the unknown possibilities posed by an undefined tomorrow will he or she be able to move from "what is" to "what could be." By focusing more on "why not?" than "if only…" you may surprise yourself how nicely your little world fits into the universe around you!

ESTABLISH THE FUTURE BY REALIZING YOUR POTENTIAL TO DEFINE YOUR REALITY

Our country is in the process of transforming itself from a creator of things into an incubator of ideas. While we still produce some of the highest quality products in the world, we rely upon technology and process efficiency to minimize labor costs while maximizing profitability. A higher level of education is required to fill entry-level jobs, and life-long learning has become necessary for one to retain their position. Parents and schools must help to prepare technologically competent students able to meet heightened standards of accountability and responsibility placed upon them by employers. Until we recognize that change is inevitable - realize that what once was will never again be - we will not move from our stagnant reality towards our potential destination. We will be like a sailboat mired fog, knowing we must move forward but afraid to go towards port for fear we will be dashed upon the unforgiving rocky shore.

Lost in the call for change is the definition of reality. Is the light at the end of the tunnel one of hope not yet realized or one of disaster lying in wait? Can we best enter the future by seeking what "has not yet been tried" or by dwelling upon (and then avoiding) what did not previously work? I would prefer to look back just long enough to acknowledge my shortcomings and analyze why an action may have resulted in an undesirable result before focusing on how I might move forward towards a brighter tomorrow. Understanding yesterday's mistakes helps them become no more than tomorrow's memories – dwelling upon them makes them a predictor of future action.

We thrive by learning to accept the previously unacceptable – by innovating rather than finding comfort in what always was. We once applied our "learning" to well-defined situations to resolve them in tested (and predictable) ways. Today, information is readily available to anyone – achieving success will require one to apply data in a way that expands knowledge and empowers actions used to create innovative solutions rather than performing assigned tasks. Our educational institutions must make sure students grasp core concepts and their application rather than simply memorizing answers to questions that the "real world" may never ask. We must move away from rewarding effort to recognizing accomplishment. We all have different gifts – we must embrace the ways our diverse individual perspectives can contribute to the accomplishments of the whole.

Knowledge is power that will never become actionable unless its application creates the wisdom needed to initiate change. Unless you are willing to act, you must accept whatever comes your way – reduced to accepting the inevitable rather than accomplishing the improbable. When we set our sights low – do ONLY those things we KNOW can be accomplished – we will accomplish nothing more than has already been previously achieved.

When we imagine that which is incomprehensible, seeing it as not only achievable but viewing it as a foregone conclusion, we can accomplish those things once believed to be impossible. Rather than settling for a "life as you know it," stretch your horizons beyond their comfortable limits as you redefine the future by rushing headlong towards an undefined reality. Shine through the darkness of the night, through the depths of life's storms, as you become a beacon to those seeking guidance - a point of focus to those seeking truth.

SHARE YOUR LIFE - REALIZE YOUR DREAMS

We share much with others in this life. We share the things we do, the air we breathe and the places we visit. We share our accomplishments whether they bring us success or result in failure. We share relationships and possessions. We share our thoughts when we converse. We share our families, our friends and our acquaintances with others. Sharing our workload and the results of our efforts has become the norm in business. Working as teams to share tasks that magnify our individual contributions by blending them with the unique gifts others are given to accomplish collectively much more than could have been completed on our own has become the mantra of workplace efficiency. With such an emphasis on sharing, however, what is truly "our own" in this life shared with others through common ground, shared existence and team-based accomplishments?

Dreams are thoughts not yet realized – aspirations not yet brought to fruition. Dreams are the basis of our goals and the foundation of our good intentions. We can live life without dreams but cannot embrace its full potential – become all that we can hope to be or realize all that we might wish to accomplish – without first visualizing what we want to become or what we desire to do within the lifetime. Those that identify their own aspirations and work towards those accomplishments while they benefit the greater good will not only add value to society but also open new horizons and identify new paths that can serve as stepping stones to a new and unrestrained future. To dream, however, we must be willing to move from the safety of our "present" towards the unknown opportunities of a "future" that have yet to be fully realized.

Dreams are not the "substance" of life – they are the icing on life's cake. They are not the "why" that people ask when confronted with an unknown or unanticipated situation – they are the "why not" that people willing to roll with the punches as they move forward continuously embrace. We can expect to accomplish more than others think possible only when we risk more than others think is safe or dream more than others think is practical. When we care more than others think is wise we may begin to realize that our dreams are more important than walking lockstep within the expectations of others.

While we share much in life with others, we rarely share more than the things we are able to easily do or accomplish. We are hesitant to share our fears – or to open ourselves to the possibility of failure. If we were to share our dreams with others – to both seek their assistance in accomplishing them AND to hold us responsible for bringing them to fruition – what more could we hope to realize? When we settle for that which comes to us easily, we become "adequately mediocre." Seek excellence – and personal satisfaction – by dreaming of all you could wish to be while striving to achieve all you could wish to accomplish. Rather than living the life that others might establish for you, live your dreams – risking more than others might think wise – so that you can accomplish more than others might think possible.

INTENTIONAL ACTIONS MOVE US FROM WHAT IS PROBABLE TO WHAT IS POSSIBLE

In living life, there are two paths we can take – the one less travelled or the one well defined. We can choose to follow the crowd and do what others want and expect us to do OR we can forge our own way to find what lies beyond the horizon. We can care about others or we can care about ourselves. We can acknowledge the efforts put forth by others or we can assume their results as our own. We can choose to make possible all things but unless we establish a destination before beginning our journey, how can we hope to differentiate between what is possible, impossible, or extremely tough to accomplish?

How can we move beyond "safe" when we seem always to take the easy path? When we choose to live safely within our four walls, our immediate surroundings, or our familiar environment how can we ever move from our present reality? Until we risk more than others think is safe, how can we expect to accomplish more than others think possible? We tend to get from life no more than we expect. We may not be seen as failing if we choose not to set specific goals BUT how can we realize success without first determining what we wish to accomplish? How will you know when you have arrived if you never thought about where you are going? How can you expect to succeed if you choose not to expect anything at all?

What wisdom is there in caring for ourselves when others have needs that are much more serious? We should not eliminate their shortfalls or shortcomings without expecting some sort of personal involvement, however. Is it not wise to teach others how to care for themselves so that we will not have to care for them forever? What greater gift can we give another than self-sufficiency?

How can we move beyond our present reality without first considering what is probable as we move towards what has not yet been proven possible? Life is practical – filled with actions that result in reactions and causes that bring effects. Replace the hollow satisfaction we tend to feel when chasing after (and bringing to fruition) the wishes of another with the fulfillment that comes from realizing our own dreams. Unless we act intentionally, how can we expect to accomplish anything at all – let alone more than anyone might think possible?

LET GO OF THE PAST BUT HOLD ON TO YOUR DREAMS

The worst parts of letting go of something with which you have become familiar are watching it pass through your fingers and worrying about whether it will ever return. When something that has become more important to your life than the very air you breathe floats away upon the wind – dancing just out of reach but never out of mind – you need to work relentlessly to retrieve it or seek intentionally to replace it. Regardless of how much you try to rationalize that what once was may never be again – that perhaps it should never have been in the first place – does not fill the emptiness growing within your heart when that which was is no more. Life drifts freely through the meadows of your soul seeking a return to its comfortable past when what you had slips through your hands – yet such a return is often an improbable dream.

Until you let something go – knowing that you will never again experience the stability it provided nor the comfort you found within the place you had found – you will never understand the emptiness that comes from letting go of a dream. Hope will remain, however, within the heart of a visionary soul. The emptiness that engulfs an individual when separated from a dream – or from a present reality – allows for the celebration of moments when reunited. When Hope is gone, life takes on the deathly pallor of a spirit drifting aimlessly with the wind. Without Dreams, reality can become a millstone holding you down – a weight keeping you from realizing your potential or moving towards the accomplishment of unfulfilled goals.

When you must move on – which is a reality we all face within this life – we must look to where we are going rather than dwell upon where we have been. We must seek new horizons rather than finding comfort in the dark of our past. We must embrace change as an opportunity to excel rather than seeing it as a blockade that makes our "comfortable path" impassable. Though a job change may not be what we wanted, accept the opportunity that "downsizing" presents should it come. One should retire "to" something rather than "away" from it – never running away from what you have but rather reaching for that which has not yet materialized. An empty nest should be filled with freedoms rather than with the knowledge that something "that was" will be no more. Life "as it was" should become a springboard into the future rather than a place to hide from "what could be".

Life provides us with many opportunities to create new realities. Accepting these challenges as inevitable – recognizing that the only constant in life is change – will allow us to let go of "what was" in order to grasp "what will be." Until you are able to truly take control of your destiny by walking from what was in order to run towards what has yet to be – your past that will control your life and you will never reach the dream that holds your future reality. Let go *(of your past)* as you hold on *(to your dreams)* so you can reach out towards a future that has yet to be realized.

PATHWAYS AND PASSAGES THROUGH CHANGE…

A collection of lessons dedicated to those willing to dream the impossible while seeking the improbable…

    To those willing to reach for the stars when establishing their reality…

        To those who would accept what could be as a destination rather than being content with what is…

    To those willing to innovate as they fulfill their dreams…

To those accepting the responsibility of INITIATING AND CELEBRATING CHANGE within a world that too often rewards mediocrity rather than recognizing excellence…

WHEN SHOULD WE LOOK FOR (AND TO) CHANGE?

We live in times of transition – of change from one existence to another. Is it best to seek change at any cost OR approach it with caution, looking before we leap? How much should we consider what we have before reaching for those things that have been outside of our grasp? We may not know the road upon which we wish to travel or realize a final destination in advance of our journey BUT only by acknowledging we are not where we want to be will we ever become more than we currently are. Until we actively and intentionally seek those things we have yet to achieve, we will never ever contribute beyond the level we have already attained.

Does the reason we change make a difference or should we consider any change positive? Before leaping towards change, make sure you consider what you are leaving, why you are leaving it, what you wish to accomplish and how you plan to proceed. Think about the positive AND the potentially negative ramifications of change. Decide whether the unknown to which you gravitate is truly a better place to be than the comfortable place you have come to know and love before you jump as acting without passion is often worse than deciding not to act at all. Consider the following when seeking personal or professional change:

• *LOOK TO BUILD UPON THE STRENGTHS YOU HAVE – THE THINGS YOU ENJOY DOING WITHIN YOUR PRESENT SITUATION – BEFORE TRYING TO ELIMINATE THOSE THINGS YOU SIMPLY DO NOT ENJOY.* When discussing change, many say their boss is intolerable, the environment oppressive, the work is not what they thought, a partner is not what he/she once was – the list is endless. Unless one seeks to identify (and accept) his or her role in each negative, however, it is difficult to create lasting change by running from a bad experience. Before blaming someone else for a bad situation, examine what role YOU may have played in its becoming tarnished and consider how YOU might be able to help restore the luster. Whenever you feel "the other side is greener," consider that you once thought you were on "the green side." Identify not only "what changed" but also "what was right in the first place."

• *IDENTIFY YOUR STRENGTHS WHEN CONSIDERING CHANGE.* Few people dwell upon what they like most about their situation – rather they carry on endlessly about what is "bad" about it. If seeking a new job, people tend to seek positions having a similar title. Individuals able to accomplish change tend to identify and build upon their proven abilities as they transition from one place to the next, leveraging what they HAVE rather than dwelling upon what they do not have or wish to achieve. If seeking change, identify the strengths that have contributed to past successes then leverage them to create different opportunities or accomplish new things.

• *ISOLATE (AND ADDRESS) THE NEGATIVES WITHIN YOUR CURRENT SITUATION TO AVOID BUILDING THEM INTO YOUR NEXT OPPORTUNITY.* We often find the things we dislike most have little to do with our duties, responsibilities or actual day-to-day activities. Many times the "things" driving us to distraction are environmental, people we work with, the level of responsibility (or lack of responsibility) we are given (or assume), the boss, the lack of attention we are receiving (without thought about the fulfillment we receive) – the list of "dislikes" could go on forever. If these are the reasons for change, make sure to resolve them before transitioning to something else. Before taking action to disrupt your existence, make sure that it needs disrupting! A relatively minor issue should not force you into giving something up that you otherwise enjoy.

Change often requires you to take the "road less traveled" if you wish to arrive at a location with which you are unfamiliar doing things you have never done in order to complete something you have not yet accomplished. We are often more comfortable doing what we have always done – and blaming others for what is not to our liking. Those seeking change must act intentionally to do things in a manner that will allow for alternative results.

When seeking change it is important that we run towards opportunity rather than away from failure. We tend to see the neighbor's "greener grass" as we ignore our own lawn's possibilities. We see the results of another's effort before fully investigating our own potential. The precursor of change should be determining what you like most about what you are now doing and building upon that foundation. Change ONLY when you are willing to walk away from the world as you know it to enter into one where you can but imagine what we will find.

INFLUENCING AND MOTIVATING OTHERS TO SUCCEED

Whether managing people, relationships, situations, teams, products, processes, your temper or yourself, someone has written a book guaranteed to make you an expert. Since there are far fewer managers than people being managed in this world, however, I've often wondered why so little attention has been given to influencing "from the bottom up" rather than to managing from "the top down." Keys to making yourself more influential would include:

- ***Recognize it is your responsibility to SELL an idea, NOT someone else's responsibility to BUY the concept.*** Good salespeople identify and relate to the needs of the buyer, not their own needs. While making a sale will obviously benefit the seller, a buyer must recognize why he or she will benefit from his or her buying decision before a sale will ever be consummated. Remain positive and upbeat, focusing on what YOU can do to "make things right" rather upon what others could do to make things fail. Until you truly "sell" change, you will be but an implementer rather than an initiator.

- ***Consider how change will impact "the whole" rather than how it might advance your personal objectives.*** Since most people are hesitant to abandon the status quo, if you want something to be different than it is, you must convince others that the promises of change are better than the comforts of staying the same. In order to initiate change, every individual must take full responsibility for being understood. If you wish to influence another's actions you must clearly demonstrate how resultant change will positively impact that individual, the organization, their environment, and their future

- *Present a realistic cost-benefit analysis of your idea as you define and communicate value.* Whether it be a major corporate decision or a family vacation, be prepared to have a realistic discussion on the cost of change as well as the results of change. Acknowledge that implementing your idea will probably mean that someone else's idea was not used. Recognize that whenever anything has changed in history, the benefits of change have outweighed the costs. It is your job to clearly communicate this if you expect to be heard.

- *When a conclusion is reached, whether or not you fully agree with it, adopt the final decision as your own.* Many ineffective influencers will "own" decisions with which they agree and "credit others" with the ones they may not have wholeheartedly supported. Remember that you will not always "win" when influencing upwards, but you will gain tremendous credibility if, after all the discussions and debates, you "own" any solution that is not illegal, unethical or immoral. We can always live to fight another day as long as we don't impale ourselves upon the sword of principle today.

- *NEVER advance an idea without having a sincere belief it will make a difference...regardless of who might receive the credit.* If we lose sight of the result of our ideas, focusing instead on getting credit for the concept, we often discredit others to make ourselves come out on top. When we consciously make others feel that they are right or responsible, rather than continually elevating ourselves into a role of infallibility, our ideas have a better chance of implementation. Assuring our desired results are realized will provide for better long-term rewards than will being recognized for short-term contributions.

- *Rather than focusing on what has (or has not) happened, dream about what has yet to occur.* Far too many individuals are haunted by what went wrong... losing sight of what went right...as their ideas come to fruition. When we are mired in a world of failure we cannot possibly reach out towards success. When we focus on "what did not happen" it is difficult to consider what could still be done differently to alter results before they become "final." When we accept "what is" we cannot realize "what could be."

We all invest tremendously in the acquisition of knowledge. Until we learn to sell our ideas, however, rather than expecting others to simply buy them from us, our knowledge will never be leveraged into positive change. We must look forward rather than backwards…convincing others to travel along the winding road with us…if we ever expect to influence change. We must acknowledge that we are capable of achieving more than we might think possible (as long as we are willing to invest our time, talent and abilities into realizing the transition) if we expect to initiate change.

It is not enough to recognize change is needed for us to become all that we might wish to be. We must understand the ramifications of complacency (as well as the rewards of transformation) and the gains of doing something (which must be greater than the pains of doing nothing) if we are to grow and succeed (or influence and motivate others to thrive). We will never be able to encourage others to grow unless (and until) we recognize our own potential.

EMBRACING CHANGE

Their aimless wanderings lay behind them…
> ***Their paths weaving desperately through the wilderness…***
>> ***Coming near then veering away…never quite crossing or becoming one.***

They stood at a crossroads…
> ***Looking back in an attempt to see how their lives had unfolded…***
>> ***Looking ahead towards a future not yet defined.***

Increasingly tired of their struggles within a thankless world…
> ***They sought a path that would lead towards truth…***
>> ***An obscure trail that would carry them to a brighter future…***

Deliberately they turned, moving forward into the vast unknown…
> ***Leaving behind the comfort and security their past once held…***
>> ***Intentionally embarking upon a path that would change their lives forever…***

An excerpt from Life's Path to the Promise of a Dream, a book of poems by Dave Smith

Why do people seek change? What makes us decide to do things differently – particularly if the things we are doing provide us comfort or bring us success? What makes us wander from "the familiar" in search of unknown opportunities? With summer's passing and a new, hectic fall upon us, we all tend to seek different ways of doing things - resolving to change in ways that will allow us more free time, success or tangible rewards.

Several factors come into play as we move beyond "where we are" to "where we might wish to be." We must recognize that before we can move from "what we have" to "what we hope for," one journey must end before another can begin – that before we can wrestle with new opportunities we must free ourselves from the constraints (and restrictions) of the old. We must acknowledge that before we can take a new path to an unknown destination we must abandon the old and familiar roads that have taken us safely to the places in which we have found comfort. All change begins with the deliberate consideration of an intentional action that, if acted upon, will forever alter where we are as it redefines where we are going (one cannot do the same things they have always done and expect different results).

Success often follows change. When we are able to produce results that were previously thought to be impossible by doing things not previously considered, those around us often view us as being "successful." Everyone desires success BUT an individual must work to accomplish something not yet done, dreamed of or considered if he or she seeks to claim the results as a personal achievement. We cannot grant success to another because it is different for everyone – one person's idea about a "logical conclusion" could be another's definition of a "good starting point." Unless (and until) we determine where we wish to "end" our journey, it is difficult to know how far we have come (or if, indeed, we have even begun to initiate a transition). Holding on to past success, however – riding a single success beyond its effective lifespan by thinking "our way" is the only way – will almost always force us to change (by revealing the shortcomings of our established approach) or disrupt our stagnant but comfortable existence (by offering a more exciting option).

We must actively appraise the things we do if we wish to remain vibrant and relevant. By continuously analyzing our strengths and weaknesses – leveraging those that pull us forward while addressing those that hold us back – we will remain effective. Recognizing that the only constant in life is change will allow us to accept the possibility of failure (and the learning it brings). Success does not come, however, from frantic movement without direction or purpose - we must intentionally stop what we are doing if we wish to start something else! To initiate change (and achieve PERSONAL success), we must intentionally address three major issues:

- *WE MUST ACT* by acknowledging where we have been, recognizing what we have done, and wishing to be (or achieve) something different before we can start travelling upon a new path. How can we better serve our customers? What can we do to improve a relationship? Must we alter our behavior so that we can remain relevant within a changing world? When our goals change we must step from our original path onto a new (perhaps uncharted) trail – must leave our comfortable surroundings in search of a new place of shelter – if we are to achieve success through refocused and redirected efforts.

- *WE MUST STOP DOING THE THINGS WE HAVE ALWAYS DONE* – no matter how effective they may have been in the past – if we seek something different results. While identifying what must be done to create meaningful change, paths (and methods) needing abandonment will inevitably be revealed, but they will not lead us anywhere until we choose to step forward. Can a worker that values time off from work (new life balance issues) be effectively disciplined with suspension (old "rules are rules" mentality)? Can an individual communicate effectively without embracing technology and learning how to "entertain" using Power Point? Can two people maintain a meaningful relationship if neither is willing to "walk a mile" in the other's shoes – or to talk about what the other might need?

- ***WE MUST IDENTIFY AND ABANDON THE THINGS THAT HOLD US BACK*** while we continue doing things that initiate change (while producing growth). We all have personal strengths – characteristics responsible for the successes we have achieved. Everyone can celebrate a "peak of accomplishment" in their past but far too many choose to dwell within the quiet valleys surrounding their peak rather than seeking new heights that rise all around them. In order to realize meaningful change we must continue doing the things that brought us to our heights while discarding those that bring us to our knees. We must seek alternative paths that will lead us forward rather than continuing to fall back upon the "safe roads" that lead to places (activities and relationships) we have already achieved or established.

People must change more than their outward appearance if they expect their path to shift significantly. We often hear about "new and improved" products only to find nothing but the packaging has changed. Television networks frequently move a failing show from one night to another in order to gain viewers from a less competitive offering. If we are resolved to change we must consciously decide NOT to "stay the course" by intentionally seeking a new path into an unknown wilderness. While we must acknowledge our past (both the wins and the losses) before we can define our present (from which we must move forward) if we harbor any expectation of creating a different future, we must choose to move from the safety that our current situation provides if we are to experience anything new.

MUCH CAN BE ACCOMPLISHED WITHOUT RUNNING AWAY

Far too many people think that moving away from a situation – that picking up and starting over – is all they need to do to begin a new life and experience different results given the same effort. They feel that changing the environment around will drastically alter their lives – will magically cause them to react differently to situations or choose different courses of action. Not surprisingly, when individuals run away from their worlds they rarely run away from themselves (so "picking up and starting over" accomplishes very little).

People tend to maximize the impact others have on their failures while minimizing their own contribution to negative results. Likewise, they maximize their personal contributions towards any success while discounting the contribution of others. They DO NOT realize that distancing themselves from a situation or problem does nothing to eliminate one of the major factors that are tough to run from – that being the person they see whenever they look in a mirror. We can run from places, situations, relationships and the ramifications of the choices we make but we cannot alter "who we are" or how we react by simply positioning ourselves in a different space or time. When recognizing the need for change and identifying the steps needed to implement it, "the monster in the closet" that needs addressing is often "us" (and the things we do) rather than "them" (or the things done to us). Identifying and owning our own role in creating a roadblock to success is vital if we are to overcome the obstacles in front of us. Realistically establishing what role we played in the success of an endeavor (rather than claiming all the credit while shifting all the blame) will help build "transferable problem solving skills" that will serve us well.

Too many people live in a world of "what is" rather than in one of "what if." They like to make excuses for things that happen "to them" rather than identifying and implementing solutions that change or alter "where they are" so they can become "what they wish to be." Nobody is going to make us succeed – we must wrap success around ourselves by considering the ramifications of each action we take and the impact that each choice we make has on the world around us. We cannot run away from "who" we are – we only shift "what" we are to a new location UNLESS we identify our strengths (and utilize them) as well as our weaknesses (and work on them) so we can own the solutions that are developed through the contributions of many (rather than through our own limited knowledge). Though a new environment might provide a fresh perspective, it will not change what we do or how we do it UNTIL we identify our flaws and intentionally act to change (or overcome) them. We cannot become something different by moving to a new location, beginning a new relationship or taking a new job unless we change, alter or modify ourselves in such a manner that new initiatives and altered perspectives are probabilities rather than remote possibilities.

Change can be good (if it is intentional rather than accidental and responsive or anticipatory rather than reactive) but we should never "change for change sake." Before running where brave men refuse to walk we should ask WHY we wish to move, WHAT we plan to do upon arrival and HOW those actions, thoughts or attitudes will be different than the ones we chose to leave behind. People cannot be "something different" by simply changing their environment – they must change who and what they are (along with where they choose to exist) if a "fresh start" is to occur. We must be unafraid to be different - to stand out from the crowd - if we seek to initiate change. A change in perspective allows for the creation of new thoughts, concepts and processes while a change of environment only provides new grounds upon which old ideas can be planted.

Change does not come easily – we must intentionally invest ourselves if different results are expected – results that cannot occur if we are doing things the same way we always have done them (even if it might be in a different location). Words describe what one wishes to accomplish - actions (and results) define success.

MOVING FORWARD REQUIRES LETTING GO

Why is it that when "all has been said and all has been done," many continue to seek what more they might say and what else they can accomplish? They seem unwilling to close the door – to move on once a decision has been made – continuously second guessing themselves to the point that "all that was said" becomes meaningless noise and "all that was done" loses its significance. When you feel that "all has been said," quit speaking and start acting. When you sense that "all has been done," turn away from the closed doors so you can begin opening new ones.

It is never wrong to change your mind or shift direction IF the conditions or factors that led to your decision change. It IS wrong to avoid making a decision or setting a course of action because you fear you may have to change your mind. When we become paralyzed by our analysis of a situation – unable (or unwilling) to accept the validity of our thought processes once an issue has been identified and a resolution formulated – we establish insurmountable roadblocks that prevent us from moving or doing anything. We become pawns to the process rather than stewards of the solution. We become bound by a need for absolute certainty, losing sight of the possibility that "a fix has been found" allowing us the freedom to consider new opportunities and challenges. When we focus on finality rather than simply seeking closure, we stifle our ability to innovate. We limit our ability to take calculated risks that may open new doors when we exerting all our energy nailing shut the doors behind us. We must shift our vision forward if we wish to let go of the past so we can move ahead into the future – allowing ourselves the luxury of turning around to face forward rather than walking backwards towards an unseen cliff.

In order to thrive we must learn to innovate rather than finding comfort in what always was (because it may never again be)! We must learn to think of alternatives (rather than simply "doing what is expected") if we wish to taste success. We must apply our knowledge to new situations rather than memorizing answers to questions that have already been (or may never be) asked. When all is said and done, our emphasis must be on recognizing accomplishment rather than rewarding effort – or people around us will continue to try proven solutions rather than accomplishing great things.

Everyone wants "change" but few take the time to define what "change" truly entails. What lies ahead for us? Is the light at the end of the tunnel one of Hope or is it one of unavoidable Disaster? Listening to promises of change is never a bad thing in and of itself. Such promises, however, should always identify what is being targeted AND what the alternative will be. Seeking change just to alter the present is hollow unless we know – and are willing to accept – the alternative opportunities available when we decide to change (OR the consequences that will necessarily follow should we NOT change).

Before accepting the premise "all that could possibly be spoken has been said and all that could be accomplished has been done," think about what might be possible (rather than dwelling upon those things that have already been accepted as feasible or worrying about things that may not work). Identify where you want to be – intentionally thinking about what must be changed (and what should be left the same) – before seeking the promise an unrealized future may hold (or worse, accepting only the reality of an already fulfilled past). Embrace the opportunities that an uncertain future offers, moving deliberately forward in an effort to grow from them, rather than worrying about things you cannot control or obsessing over change that is going to happen regardless of what you may (or may not) do.

Individuals either embrace the opportunity of a new tomorrow by consciously (and intentionally) leaving behind what is not working as they seek what might work OR they are swept up in someone else's vision without thinking about its ramifications. Do not fear change – fear only those things AND individuals that refuse to change as you seek to expand your present-day reality into a fresh new tomorrow. Closing one door usually opens another – but it does not eliminate the opportunity to reopen the door should situations change. All may never be said – and all may never be done – but we all should recognize and acknowledge "stopping points" from which we can move forward if we ever hope to hear what has yet to be said or experience what has not yet been accomplished.

<u>RESOLVING TO CHANGE</u>

The only certainty about change is that it will happen – regardless of what we do or say. We can anticipate change – planning alternative reactions to the multitude of possibilities that might present themselves – but rarely can we predict with any degree of accuracy what we will be doing next year – or even tomorrow. Change is far too elusive to be contained – its possibilities far too numerous to be compartmentalized within our finite minds. In order to accomplish change we must act with purpose, refuse to accept the status quo – constantly identifying new possibilities through a process of screening or validating their potential benefit by measuring their rewards against the investment of time and effort required to bring them to fruition.

As we move from one year to the next, many make definitive resolutions of what they wish to change – proclaiming what will be different or what things in life they will leave behind – without ever taking the time to identify what must be changed BEFORE they move forward. They often fail to realize their dreams because they do not identify and eliminate the behaviors that led to the need for change. We cannot expect to see different results until we start doing things, thinking about our capabilities or reacting differently to the stimuli around us. Change is as much about identifying where we want to MOVE FROM as it is about looking towards where we wish to be. We need to establish goals and objectives in order to begin a journey towards change – but to accomplish change we must intentionally decide to move away from our past without becoming comfortable OR fearful within the "present" we find if we wish to embrace all the future might hold.

We must come to grips with who we are and what we do well if we seek lasting change. We must embrace our positive attributes while alienating the negative – and accept that where we wish to be IS an extension of where we are rather than a foreign soil or a different planet. Change most often succeeds when it is gradual – when it builds from our strengths while minimizing our weaknesses – rather than proclaiming that things will be different without planning, preparation or self-awareness. We can initiate and maintain change that builds upon what we do well – that does not require a complete transformation of who we are or what we portray ourselves to be. It is relatively easy to change when we can alter a negative behavior or isolate a wandering thought to receive a greater reward than we would have had if we remained tied to what we did or where we were. Self-directed change can be accomplished when the initiator of change is able to monitor progress, see results and continue to move forward because the positive benefits gained are greater than those received had change NOT been initiated. Typically, resolutions that result in visible physical or behavioral change that others notice and comment upon passively feed one's desire to maintain their change. When obvious "positives" come from minor behavioral changes or altered choices, resolutions are often at least partially (if not fully) realized.

Other resolutions, however, while initiated through internal desires (one must WANT to change before change can occur) may need external oversight to keep the train on the track and moving in the right direction. It is almost impossible to "resolve" to be something different or "wake up" as someone other than who we have always been without some kind of outside accountability. Far too often when we make a personal commitment to alter our behavior we compromise our internal standards when "the going gets tough" by allowing ourselves to "stop going." We accept a level of "sameness" when we measure our results and answer only to ourselves. While short-term change can be dictated, lasting change occurs ONLY when we internally formulate the "what", fully realize the "why," understand the "how" and are fully committed to the "what will be." Relying upon a trusted friend, partner or co-worker to discuss the distractions while holding us accountable to push forward will help us make significant and lasting change. We must declare these resolutions publicly (even if the "public" to whom we declare them is but one or two) rather than keeping them secret IF we truly want help in our accomplishing transformational change.

Whenever you resolve to change, take the time to start fresh BUT hold on to those things that you do well – that move you forward – rather than seeking only to be drastically different. Change is good – but sometimes choosing NOT to change can be just as rewarding. Do not, however, accept mediocrity as a standard while finding comfort in complacency. When you resolve to change, do whatever it takes (internally OR with an external accountability partner) to initiate, monitor and maintain the new direction or you will never reach a new plateau.

CREATING (OR ALLOWING) BEHAVIORAL CHANGE

There are three ways we can try to change another's behavior. We can order someone to change, enforcing the altered behavior with penalties or threats (coercion). We can provide a reward or some other external recognition that is of value to them should they change (motivation). We can provide a path that will make them a better person or allow them to be something different than they are (inspiration). Whether in a business or personal relationship – or any role in which we find ourselves interacting with another in order to accomplish a single objective – positive and meaningful change results from an intentional action (even if one intentionally decides not to act) rather than an accidental happenstance.

Supervisors often coerce individuals to change. They issue orders, give directions and tell people what to do (and often how to do it). Theirs can often be a world having few opportunities for independent action so they provide even fewer chances for people they supervise to act independently. While supervision IS (thankfully) changing, many individuals leading work that can be accomplished without much training or preparation spend much of their time assigning work, reviewing processes and measuring results, leaving little time to invest on motivating or influencing altered behavior. Rather than asking or laying the groundwork for change, they direct and monitor activities so they can achieve on a personal level but often negate individuality when coercing change. In personal relationships, individuals who coerce others often tear them down to build themselves up, focusing on "what went wrong" rather than celebrating "what went well." Coercive individuals tend to get what they want but may get ONLY what they want, with their gains being short term and of limited value. Telling someone how to do something produces quick and focused activity but rarely the best possible results.

Managers often motivate individuals to change. They identify alternatives, provide choices and give people reasons that make them want to alter their behavior. When combined with punishment for not changing, motivation can be a powerful means of producing results. The problem with motivation, however, is that an external force must initiate the change. In a working relationship, a manager often identifies what is best for all involved parties then initiates action by spelling out what will happen if change does not occur (coercion) but also what will happen should favorable change occur (motivating the alteration). As long as a manager is present to identify a suspect behavior and provide reason to change, good things will happen. Rarely, however, will an employee used to constant motivation see the need to change unless they continue to receive external impetus. Much can be accomplished when individuals are motivated to change – the problem with motivation, however, is that an object at rest (or an individual whom is content to do what he or she is doing) tends to remain at rest (or doing what has proven to be comfortable). Until one is convinced that they must change their behavior if they are to receive different results, they will not experience growth.

Leaders inspire others to change. Rather than telling people what must be done they show individuals a better way. Rather than dwelling upon an individual's negative behavior they reward positive efforts. Leaders paint a picture of "what if" or "what could be" rather than one of "what is" or "what will always be." A leader makes people want to change in order to achieve something they wish to have, accomplish or become. Inspirational change goes beyond telling (coercion) and past selling (motivation) – it leads another towards self-actualization. Inspiration causes people to see why changes should take place, creating an internal desire to abandon who they are to become what awaits them. Inspirational change is often caused by one's desire to "be like" another or to achieve what someone else has accomplished – to make oneself (or another) proud of their actions. In a personal relationship, inspirational leadership makes another want to join in (rather than follow) and to share the "road less traveled" (rather than taking the quickest, fastest route to nowhere). Rarely will inspirational leaders tell another what must be done or how to do it – they allow their actions to speak louder than their words. When we look to be that which has not yet been identified we initiate lasting change – which becomes the platform for continued growth.

Whether you choose to coerce, motivate or inspire change, recognize that an individual must see a reason to change before they will abandon their ways to pursue a new horizon. We cannot CREATE change within an individual – we are only able to initiate it. We cannot FORCE change within an individual – we are only able to guide it. We cannot make another do that which they choose not to – we can only provide positive reasons to act AND identify negative consequences should one choose not to act appropriately.

TURN! TURN! TURN! – ALL CHANGE BEGINS WITH AN END

The sequence of words within the lyrics of a '60's era song ("Turn, Turn, Turn" by The Byrds) are rearranged from their original order but taken almost verbatim from Ecclesiastes Chapter 3 – traditionally ascribed to King Solomon. Far too often we see life as a series of dead ends, lost opportunities and hidden darkness rather than emerging light shed upon unlimited potential. The song, often used to promote peace while denouncing war during the Vietnam era, tells us there is…

- *A time to be born, and a time to die; a time to plant, a time to reap that which is planted*
- *A time to kill, and a time to heal; a time to break down, and a time to build up*
- *A time to weep, and a time to laugh; a time to mourn, and a time to dance*

- *A time to get, and a time to lose; a time to keep, and a time to cast away*
- *A time to rend, and a time to sow; a time to keep silence, and a time to speak*
- *A time to cast away stones, and a time to gather stones together*
- *A time to embrace, and time to refrain from embracing*
- *A time to love, and a time to hate; a time of war, and a time of peace, and, above all*
- *To everything there is a season, and a time to every purpose under the heavens*

I recognize that I think differently than most so should not be surprised that, among other thoughts and emotions, these words came crashing down upon me recently as I wandered through a large retail store about to close. The nearly empty racks – their substance stripped from them by customers eager to find a bargain – stand as barren as the carcass of a living creature pounced upon by scavengers seeking sustenance. The organization – once a provider of jobs for many – is but a final resting place for the few left behind to shutter its doors. The sight of an enterprise shutting saddens me because it brings to an end what were once fresh starts and new beginnings – darkening the bright promise of a dream as it mirrors the finality changing seasons bring as the time progresses.

In our personal relationships or the business interactions in which we participate, we need not dwell upon the loss each season's passing brings for within each end we are offered hope of a new beginning. We can hold on to what will no longer be OR reach out to identify new dreams that will provide us with an opportunity to succeed anew. We can stay silent in our suffering as we mourn the past or speak out in anticipation of those things that have yet to be realized. We can cast away those things holding us back or gather up new opportunities upon which we can establish a new foundation. Our perspective determines how we embrace opportunities in life – how we "Turn, Turn, Turn" when given the chance to begin anew – and what will become of our dreams and aspirations as we move forward towards each new beginning.

The closing of a business can be much like the end of a relationship. No matter how much we may seek comfort in "what was" we cannot hide from the fact that changing seasons bring new tomorrows – an unknown that can result in either crippling anxiety or exhilarating opportunity. Our world is filled with choices that bring us new beginnings – that allow us to either "keep or to cast away" as we "plant or reap." It is up to us to make the most of our opportunities – to continue turning from one to the next – if we are to thrive in the life we have been given.

Make the most of your life as you "Turn, Turn, Turn" from the close of each seemingly final chapter towards the opportunities you will find if you but open your eyes to the potential within each new horizon!

IMPLEMENTING CHANGE

What makes us decide to do things differently – particularly if the things we are doing provide us comfort or a measure of success? What makes us wander from what is familiar to us in search of unknown opportunities? If we wish to move beyond our current station in life – expecting something different to result from our actions and choices – we must start by deliberately considering of an intentional act that, when taken, will forever change us. When we consider the ramifications of changed behavior and act to implement change we redefine where we are going (one should not expect similar results when doing things differently) by intentionally altering where we have been and what we have done while moving relentlessly towards where we want to be.

Far too often success breeds arrogance, which leads to complacency. If we ride a single success beyond its effective lifespan – thinking "our way" is the only way – someone else will either assume our market share (by improving upon what we do), force us to change (by revealing the shortcomings of our established approach), or disrupt our stagnant but comfortable existence (by offering a more exciting option). We must actively appraise the things we do – both within our work and our personal relationships – retaining those things that contribute to our growth and replacing those that hold us back. By continuously analyzing both our strengths and weaknesses, identifying the things that hold us back and leveraging those that pull us forward, we can remain an effective contributor to the life around us.

Recognizing that change is the only constant in life is necessary if we are to enjoy the rewards that come from accepting the risks of change. We must learn to embrace the possibility of failure – recognizing that with failure comes learning which leads to growth. Success is not born through frantic movement without direction or purpose. It comes ONLY when we stop what we are doing – when we consider the many paths upon which we could travel – so we can begin doing something new by taking a new road in a different direction.

Whenever we initiate change, we must recognize and acknowledge three major factors - intentionally identifying and addressing their hold upon us:

- ***We must acknowledge where we have been, recognize what we have accomplished, and wish to be or do something different before we can start to travel upon a new path.*** How can we better serve our customers? What can we do to improve a relationship? Must we alter our behavior so that we can remain relevant within a changing world? Is there anything that we can do to strengthen another – or that we would be willing to allow another do to help strengthen us? We recognize the need for change when our goals or objectives have changed. We must consciously step from our original path onto one that will refocus and redirect our efforts if we wish to harvest the fruits of change. Before embarking on such a path, however, internalize that our desire to begin something new is stronger than our contentment with what we have – that moving forward provides more desirable rewards than remaining where we are.

- ***We must stop doing the things we are doing – that we have always done - no matter how effective they may have been in the past or how comfortable we might be in doing them.*** When we accept and acknowledge that change is necessary we must abandon the paths (and methods) with which we are comfortable, intentionally and deliberately walking away from the safety provided. A change in paradigm must often occur – walking away from "what is usually done and accepted by others" towards "what has not yet been tried." A disciplinary procedure must not always include time off without pay (what is the value of suspension when an employee chooses not to work in the first place?). A relationship must provide all involved with a measure of satisfaction – building the esteem of all parties – or it is nothing more than a hollow structure built on shifting sand. How can a meaningful relationship be maintained if both parties want everything "their way" with neither willing to "walk a mile" in the other's shoes?

- ***As we identify and abandon the habits and actions holding us back we must move forward in a way that produce positive growth and change – that rewards us for our efforts so that we will continue to reach for new horizons.*** We all have personal strengths – the characteristics responsible for any success we have achieved. Everyone can celebrate "peaks of accomplishment" in their past. Far too many, however, choose to rest within the quiet valleys beyond their achievements, gazing up and establishing value based on those things that were done in the past rather than on those things that have not yet been identified. In order to realize meaningful change we must identify the thoughts, practices and action that brought us to our heights (to replicate them) while discarding those that brought us to our knees (to avoid their recurrence).

People must change more than their outward appearance if they expect their path to shift significantly. We often hear about "new and improved" products only to find nothing but the packaging has changed. Television networks frequently change the night that a failing program airs in order to gain viewers from a less competitive offering. If we are resolved to change we must consciously decide NOT to "stay the course" by innovatively clearing a new path into an unknown wilderness. We must acknowledge our past (both the wins and the losses) before we can define our present (from which we must move forward) if we harbor any expectation of creating a different future (that holds limitless opportunity). In order to initiate change it is important that we continually take stock of what we are doing and where we are going – then actively seek paths that will lead us from complacency to new destinations, new relationships and new opportunities. When we come to a fork in the road we must move forward rather than waiting for someone else to determine our path. Once we identify our new direction we must resolve to move forward – for nothing will change until we consciously and intentionally move from where we are towards where we wish to be.

TRANSFORMATIONAL WISDOM: INTENTIONALLY APPLYING KNOWLEDGE IN PURSUIT OF TRUTH

Today's world is afloat with facts, data and information yet it seems that problem-solving skills are slipping through our hands like an ice cube melting within our grasp. We read newspapers (sometimes), watch news (occasionally), page through magazines and check out our electronic resources constantly – knowing what is happening (almost before it happens!) throughout the world. We know if a disaster has occurred, if the price of gas is about to rise, what is happening in Washington (though a "still shot" could probably capture political activity as well as a news clip!) and who just won a ballgame BUT we have difficulty readily applying our wealth of knowledge to un-related circumstances.

Many can memorize facts but far too few can ask the "right questions" that would allow for the formation of a "best" solution when presented with a new challenge. We often seek answers before fully formulating a question. We want answers – NOW – without a moment's hesitation. We seek stories with tightly wound endings rather than events that have yet to unfold. We find interest in other's problems – reinforcing the fact that "good news does not sell." We accept another's interpretation of the facts as being "gospel truth" rather than digging into a story and coming to our own conclusions. We want to be entertained (rather than informed), agreed with (rather than challenged) and provided for (rather than providing for others). It seems that the application of information to create a viable solution – taking the risk required to make a difference by being different – is no longer a desirable characteristic. Impatience and intolerance have become the driving factors in "effective" communication with the analysis of data and deliberate actions due to those findings but afterthoughts in the creation of reality.

There is no such thing as confidentiality anymore. People prefer to "share openly and honestly" everything they know (have heard or have gained knowledge about in private conversation) rather than exhibiting a "discretionary silence" in regards to conversations that could do more harm than good. Discretion was once the rule – it is now an exception to the rule. Integrity was once an integral part of an individual's make-up – it is now but an insignificant backdrop to life's everyday drama. Relationships once rooted in honesty and nurtured by unconditional love now seem built upon circumstance and fed by individual desires. In order to regain credibility we must recognize and consistently honor the privacy of others – their values, their likes, their dislikes and their preferences – rather than holding them open in every aspect like a book without a cover.

Our senses seem overly stimulated by details, information and opportunities yet we far too infrequently take the time to identify issues before moving forward with unthinking (and untenable) solutions. We run before we walk – seemingly oblivious to the fact we might fall – our impatience ruling the day. We fly rather than run – oblivious to the fact others have come before us – relegating their experiences (both wins and losses) to a silent history rather than including their insights into our ongoing thought processes. We pursue the impossible (or at least the improbable) rather than finding comfort in the reality of "what is" and extrapolating it into that which has not yet become – far too often leaping ahead without thought or direction rather than moving slowly (and steadily) forward.

It really does not matter which path you take when you are lost – when you do not know where you are going nor from what you are moving – as any progress is better than no movement at all. In order to transform knowledge into wisdom we must take the time to analyze the plethora of information around us – to make decisions count by anticipating a destination before moving from one situation to another and planning where you want to be before leaping from the frying pan into the fire. One will rarely fail if they do not establish goals – yet success hinges upon the creation and attainment of targets and the accomplishment of individual dreams. It is nearly impossible to make a poor choice or move in the "wrong direction" when one does not care where they are going nor worry about how they will get there, yet little credit can be taken for unanticipated results generated through unplanned actions.

PATHWAYS AND PASSAGES TO LEADERSHIP...

A collection of leadership lessons dedicated to those willing to dream the impossible while seeking the improbable...
  To those willing to reach for the stars when establishing their reality...
    To those who would accept what could as a destination rather than being content with what is...
  To those willing to initiate change as they fulfill their dreams...
To those acknowledging the responsibilities of LEADERSHIP within a struggling world.

A LEADERSHIP DILEMA

Our world needs strong, unwavering leadership more than ever. Parents want to be their children's friends rather than their spiritual and emotional leaders. People overlook critical issues within their relationships, preferring to avoid confrontation and resolution by staying away from each other or being too busy to talk. Partisan politicians are more committed to identifying who is at fault than to recognizing the problems and acting to resolve them. Is it possible (or even worthwhile) to differentiate "management" from "leadership?" I sometimes fear that our leaders have taken leave – or are at least staying so far below the radar screen (and out of fire) that their effectiveness may be compromised. IF that is the case, where have the leaders gone – and how can we bring them back?

If someone could develop a "one size fits all" leadership style that was "guaranteed to produce positive results" they would make a fortune. We all bring unique and individual characteristics to the leadership party so such an approach could not work. To maximize results we must identify and accentuate strengths, meld them into the fabric and culture of our workplace, then find ways to make up for our inevitable weaknesses. While this might prove to be a big challenge, several consistent differences between strong leaders and those who wish they could lead would include:

- Leaders who struggle to gain respect often "deliver" news as being "from Management" rather than "owning it" and seek credit for things that "go right" while assigning blame for things that "go wrong."

- True leaders leave their reservations about communications in the meeting room – expressing opinions and concerns behind closed doors – then take ownership for the news they deliver. They also tend to "own" their department's failures while deferring the ownership of success to others.

- Leaders who struggle to make a difference often wait for direction and guidance (so they do not do something that might be "wrong") then openly express resentment when excluded from the decision-making process. They seek recognition but avoid the ownership of failure yet the absence of their input prevents them from ever claiming the fruits of success.

- Strong leaders make decisions based on the information they have at their disposal (recognizing that if the information changes, so might their decision). They then take action, guiding employees towards the accomplishment of a goal AND informing top management (not necessarily seeking permission) of their progress.

- Ineffective leaders tend to ask, "Why am I not part of the management team?" Strong leaders step forward to make themselves an invaluable part of the team by learning as much about the organization as possible and leveraging this knowledge to make significant, profitable decisions.

While managers are often appointed, promoted or anointed, leaders assume responsibility through their actions and gain credibility through an honest and unwavering expression of their character. A manager may assign blame – a leader assumes it. A manager often deflects criticism – a leader addresses it. A Manager can lead but tends to focus on how things "must be done" rather than on what "must be accomplished." Putting his or her own needs above those of others, a manager often creates a sense of "having to do work" through fear of the consequences rather than creating an environment that encourages others to perform.

Leaders typically demonstrate the ability to influence by example to gain the support of others that choose to follow. They pull others up while rising to the top rather than climbing on top of them as if they were rungs on a ladder. Leaders understand their "audience" when speaking or communicating – incorporating the needs and desires of the group into the message delivered and the results expected. Leaders recognize there is no limit as to how much can be accomplished IF they do not care who receives the credit for the work being done. Further, great leaders put more effort into selling than they do into telling – into securing "buy-in" and sharing ownership than they do making excuses or assigning blame. They tend to recognize that people (both in the workplace AND within society) contribute more if they WANT to do something than if they HAVE to do something.

Our region needs confident, competent leaders willing to take risks and to grow from their consequences. We need fair and honest individuals willing to lead by example rather than by edict – seeking to motivate rather than intimidate. Are you a part of the solution or are you a major part of the problem? Do you anticipate "what might happen" and prepare for it or react to "what has happened" by blaming others rather than accepting the consequences? Do your actions inspire others to action or encourage them to conspire against you? A society that expects others to "do as I say rather than as I do" is one that may "get by" but will rarely thrive.

Where have the leaders gone? Look in the mirror! We all lead someone or something, be it a business, a family or simply our own existence. Let your intentional actions reflect positively upon someone else as you fulfill your own destiny. When individuals receive the tools with which to work (education, experience and/or mentoring) and the environment in which to operate (honest, open, accepting and forgiving) with leadership that encourages growth, there will be no limit to our possibilities.

ARE MANAGEMENT AND LEADERSHIP THE SAME?

Management is the ability to transform one person's talents into performance. Good managers identify each individual's unique talents and abilities. They treat people EQUITABLY rather than EQUALLY – determining what is best for them based on their abilities and how they can contribute most rather than assuming all should receive equal benefits even if they do not add similar value. Good managers define and communicate expectations, then assign tasks to persons having the greatest potential for success – giving them the ability to act independently and the right to assume responsibility for results.

Experienced managers leverage individual talent and experience towards the successful accomplishment of organizational goals and objectives – identifying existing abilities and maximizing contributions by assigning duties and managing priorities RATHER THAN focusing on training individuals to "fix" their shortcomings. While training is critical and often necessary, it should not be seen as the "ends" but rather as the "means." Recognizing that all employees contribute differently, and accepting that individual contributions are a necessary part of success, helps to define a great manager. A good manager might try to elevate all employees to their highest potential. A great manager will utilize an employee's inherent ability to accomplish great things. Should employees need additional training, a great manager will know how each employee learns best and set up programs that cater to individual needs and differences.

Leadership is moving people (as opposed to individuals) towards a common good – rallying the team to accomplish great things together rather than capitalizing on an individual's existing talent. A leader needs to be eternally optimistic – knowing that people working together will eventually accomplish things better and more easily than those working alone. Great leaders make employees feel that anything is possible – that no mountain is too high to climb and no valley too deep to enter – by "showing the way" rather than providing tools for them to move forward by themselves. Leaders demonstrate what must be done and accomplished rather than by telling them and staying out of the way.

Leaders motivate through actions rather than through words and assignments as they join in to make sure the team accomplishes things as a cohesive and collaborative body rather than as a group of talented individuals. Great leaders communicate clearly by defining expectations and focusing on anticipated results as they motivate individuals to work with others to maximize the impact of their group's efforts. Leaders live their words through their actions. Effective leaders are able to identify individual potential that can be nurtured and melded into a great functioning team. Should a team need additional training, great leaders would develop programs to teach skills that will benefit the organization rather than strengthening individual talents that already exist within the team.

Are you a Manager or a Leader? Far too often we see problems caused by well-intentioned supervisors managing when they should lead OR trying to lead when times call for strong management. A strong MANAGER tends to accomplish specific things more quickly. Tasks are clearly identified, people having proven abilities are assigned to accomplish them, and results are expected immediately. A strong LEADER will pull others towards outcomes rather than pushing them towards pre-defined destinations. A leader will draw others forward using a carrot while a manager may tend to carry (and liberally apply) a stick. Both styles are necessary (at times) in order for organizations (OR relationships) to thrive BUT there is a time and a place for each. Choose your "time and place" wisely to help maximize the results your group can achieve!

HOW CAN ONE LEAD FROM BEHIND?

I have found that several kinds of leaders exist – all effective in their own way yet all very different in the way they lead. I have seen those that lead from behind – that push others to where they wish them to be – often hiding behind the throng as if they are seeking protection from the resistance that comes when new initiatives are advanced against a traditional, "set in its ways" establishment. I have seen those that interact with their team but fail to provide direction or initiate change as they share successes and blame equally – often driving decisions down to the lowest common denominator so that no one individual will be held responsible for failure (insuring that no one individual will receive recognition or praise). I have seen those that lead from the front – that cast a vision as to where the team should go, move ahead to clear the path of potential hazards, and wait for the group to catch up before proceeding forward – living the example that they would like to see assumed by those they lead.

Leading from behind is like trying to push a string uphill. It is almost impossible to keep a string straight and moving in one direction when applying pressure from behind (unless one adds a wire or some other outside strength to keep the string from bending). Try dumping a glass of water on a marble counter and pushing it water towards a sink. The water spreads out uncontrollably in all directions, eventually making it to a final destination only after it has moved far outside of its initial path and spread far afield from its initial and inevitable end. Leading from behind is like trying to herd cats – you may move a group forward but it will be from a point of chaos rather than in a structured order – from uncontrolled havoc rather than anticipated and planned intentional actions.

Joining the group to lead is OK if you are a goose – for the lead to a migrating flock changes as if with the wind – but such interchangeable leadership is rarely synonymous with greatness within society. In order advance as a unit, someone must step away from the pack. Someone must be willing to step forward so that others might follow or the things that have always been done will continue to be accomplished (though, perhaps, more efficiently due to repetition) and the roads that have always been travelled will continue to be taken (though, perhaps, with less risk as all the twists and turns are anticipated). Pack leaders tend to hold on to security but rarely realize innovation. They tend to find comfort within their temporary "known" rather than stepping towards a yet to be defined "unknown." They may share a common goal and objective with those they lead but often find their successes are but mediocrity as they seek to avoid failure (rather than seeking to grasp success.)

Groups that move ahead as a singular unit due to the intentional actions of a leader who identifies goals, sounds the charge, then pulls the troops forward as they follow his or her lead find great success. When objectives are clearly defined and communicated - with responsibility and accountability assigned to individuals willing to embrace failures fall–out while liberally sharing the praise from success, no objective is impossible – no mountain too high to climb nor valley from which to rise. A group can model and assimilate the successful behavior of a leader much more easily than it can assume success from imposed directives coming up from the rear.

We must "lead, follow or get out of the way" as we move through life. Following rarely makes waves and does not produce new or innovative things but can accomplishes those basic things that need to be done in society that provide security, consistency and (often) rewards for those setting the goals and leading. Getting out of the way simply removes a barrier to success – it rarely allows one to enjoy individual rewards or accomplishments as stepping aside simply avoids or delays our confrontation of obstacles placed in front of us that keep us from those things we wish to achieve. Leading allows us to determine our own path – to find our own way (be it good or bad, positive or negative) as we seek to accomplish great things.

It takes a village to raise a child. Perhaps we would all be better leaders (and ultimately lead better lives) if we realized it takes more than a village – it takes the cumulative efforts of all those around us being focused into a singular point of energy – to achieve greatness. Greatness comes to those willing to lead – success often comes to those willing to learn as they follow.

PRACTICAL LEADERSHIP

True leaders emerge during times of trouble, turmoil and strife – riding the strength of their convictions to success – then thrive as conditions improve. While there should be very little difference in your leadership style when facing unexpected hurdles (whether at work or at home), far too many "competent" individuals excuse their actions (or inactivity) by blaming them on or deferring them to others. They bend to fit into their surroundings rather than standing firmly against life's storms. Seeking short term-gain (popularity, acceptance, being "liked") often damages long-term credibility (predictability, consistency, being "fair."). Some examples of BOTH an appropriate action AND a "fall back" reaction would include the following:

A company is experiencing tough economic times and has asked Management to trim expenses. Two approaches to this situation might be:

- Inform employees that cutbacks and layoffs might be necessary due to reduced sales and increased inventory. Task departments with the responsibility to find ways expenses might be cut with a minimal impact on staff by identifying productive work that could be done so that all staff can continue working while contributing to the bottom line.

- Tell staff to "look busy" because "top management" is out to cut employees and you do not want any of "your people" to be impacted. In showing compassion to employees by "building a bridge with staff based on a mutual fear of top management," this type of manager may avoid the "blame bullet" but will never earn recognition as a leader. Deferring responsibility to someone else moves an individual from being an integral part of the solution to being an expendable part of the problem.

A Leader takes ownership of his or her actions. By taking ownership of a situation rather than blaming another for an unfortunate circumstance, a good manager accepts and faces reality. He or she affirms that things are tough (most employees probably already known this and are waiting for affirmation). After stating facts, employees are asked to be involved in the development of a solution (getting "buy-in" will make even a mediocre idea achievable). Painting a realistic picture of what could happen establishes ownership of the situation and adds urgency to resolving the problem. Blaming someone else in order to remain friends or be popular is not a long-term solution. A Leader, by the very nature of his or her work, leads (if not, he or she should either follow or get out of the way!). Though accepting responsibility for decisions (even when they negatively affect the lives of others) is not always the easiest thing to do, it is always more acceptable than deferring the decision to another ("management says I have..."). Your employees may not see you as their "friend" when you personalize your supervisory responsibilities but you will earn their respect when you are fair, consistent and predictable.

An individual has made a "bad decision" that could seriously hurt another's feelings and tarnish his/her reputation with no lasting damage was done but issues of trust and credibility may be involved. There are always more than one way to address and resolve our personal failings but which of these three approaches might most match your first response (and is that the same as the "best" alternative)?

- Ignore the situation and hope it goes away. The individual whom may be harmed has not heard anything of your actions and you do not believe he or she ever will. Adhering to the tenant "if it is not broke, do not try to fix it," you walk around the elephant in the room and move on as if nothing ever happened.

- Come forward and tell part of the tale – enough to scratch the surface so if something "leaks" the person will be prepared and aware even if the full extent of the discretion has not been revealed but not enough to "spill the beans" or establish responsibility. If additional details come out you can always discount the account or blame someone else for putting you up to it. It is easier, after all, to ask forgiveness than to seek permission.

- Fall on the sword, so to speak, by telling all and resolving to change. Do not blame another – accept responsibility for your actions and deal with their repercussions. Do not needlessly or intentionally hurt another in the recounting of your tale but make sure that you have learned from your mistake so that it does not become a recurring habit.

Gaining respect and credibility is far better than trying to be a friend to those you manage. Learning how to ask the right questions when investigating a situation – then listening to hear the truthful answer – will help you see "the forest from the trees." Fools rush in – leaders learn to step back so they can ask why something was done rather than constantly pushing forward to address only what happened. A Leader takes his or her personal obligations more seriously than their work expectations. Trust cannot be exhibited for a day unless it is consistently demonstrated throughout an individual's life. While taking the easy road (ignoring a situation or partially revealing a truth) may be less painful and create fewer short-term disruptions, individuals preferring to dodge responsibility for their choices and actions will never be seen as credible leaders when they are provided the opportunity to lead. Great leaders thoughtfully and carefully consider all their decisions BEFORE they are made, making sure they are willing and able to accept the results of their actions so they can move forward with confidence to accept the rewards (or deal with the repercussions) of their actions.

We are bound to fall victim to our human vulnerabilities as we strive to become better leaders UNLESS we intentionally take the road less traveled rather than the easy. Remain true to your values – transferring the skills and aptitudes you demonstrate on a personal level to the workplace – as you say what you believe and do what you know to be right. Be the leader you were destined to become by equipping yourself with the tools necessary to accomplish the task – seeking and participating in training designed to maximize your ability to motivate others.

HUMILITY, HONESTY AND INTEGRITY - LEADERSHIP CHARACTERISTICS

Great leaders tend to display a fierce resolve to do whatever is needed in order to accomplish their stated objectives without really caring who gets the credit for the work as long as the results are achieved. If we accept this as an indicator of success, it conflicts with what we see as great qualities in the people we hold up in our traditional definition of leaders - those who "make a name for themselves" as they accomplish much (personally) while making significant changes in industry, education or society. While one person may be able to catalyze change, no one person can cause change to happen unless others are motivated to engage in and implement a change in behavior that will lead to a new result.

Most people identify great leaders as being people like Steven Jobs, Jack Welch, perhaps a President or two of the United States – identifying "leadership" with an outspoken champion of change whom has accomplished visible things through his or her actions. While these individuals may be change agents, they often use their position of power to "dictate" change rather than being an effective and humble leader able to facilitate change. Individuals able to encourage "buy in" to from others to implement change – leveraging the momentum of the whole to accomplish more than any one person could have cone – leave a truly inspirational legacy. Max DePree, a great West Michigan leader, wrote that "Leaders don't inflict pain; they bear pain." In order to lead effectively, one must consistently demonstrate humility, honesty and integrity so that people want to follow (noting that "following" should never be done blindly – it MUST include independent thought, analysis and consciously directed efforts).

Humility is disciplined strength. Humble leaders are quick to give credit and slow to accept praise. While a leader must be competitive in order to grow an organization, the manager who takes all the credit will find him/herself without a team to enact change! Think about how different a sporting event would be if the coaches took all the credit for their team's success. While chess may allow for one-on-one activity, there would not be much of a game when played if the abilities of each individual contributor were not melded into a functional unit having one purpose, mission and objective.

Honesty is living, speaking and acting with a truthful sincerity free from deceit or fraud. Communicating honestly means to speak plainly and pointedly – stating all facts and assumptions considered before making a decision – so that people know what you are saying AND (perhaps more importantly) why you are saying it. Respect is not purchased by cashing in an astounding vocabulary – it is earned by simply stating one's position so that it can be clearly understood and acted upon. While we have the right to freely and openly express our beliefs (short of harming another), we ARE NOT given the right to be taken seriously in all that we say – unless we have earned it by consistently demonstrating a high level of integrity through our actions. Unless (and until) we are seen as being dependable, credible and honest by others, we might be able to impose our will upon individuals but we will not be able to motivate, inspire or lead them towards greatness.

Integrity is the value one establishes when he or she adheres to moral and ethical principles as guiding factors in the decisions they make – when moral character and honesty is expressed within all their personal and business interactions. People respect individuals perceived as "having integrity," trusting what they say and willingly following where they lead because they know "where they are coming from" in everything that is said or done. Saying what you mean – then doing what you say – are two of the greatest attributes a leader can possess.

ACCOMPLISH MORE BY LEADING (NOT CONTROLLING) OTHERS

Great leaders develop practices and communicate expectations that allow them to manage fairly and consistently as they motivate people to contribute their proportionate share towards the success of the team or the stability of relationships. Unfortunately, there are many insecure and unprepared leaders seeking to claim all of the "gain" while accepting none of the "blame." The road to success is not a highway built by a single individual – rather it is a precarious path paved with the sacrifice and hard work of a team allowing individuals to share both setbacks and successes as they grow together towards the accomplishment of a goal.

We maximize the potential for success when a group develops and discusses mutually beneficial objectives then takes the actions necessary to bring them to fruition. Poorly thought-out initiatives, reactions without consideration of repercussions and a general misdirection of otherwise worthwhile effort will result in failure. A successful leader determines a direction, communicates a potential course of action then monitors progress – stepping in to redirect effort only when necessary. In order to accomplish much with others, a leader must:

- **_BE ACTIVELY ENGAGED IN BUILDING APPROPRIATE RELATIONSHIPS._** Successful leaders are actively involved in making the decisions that affect themselves, those around them and/or their families. Poor leaders often allow others to direct their actions (then complain when things do not progress as they might have wished). Good leaders make decisions then move forward while monitoring progress so a detour does not become a dead end. Poor leaders lose track of the "big picture" while making isolated decisions – tending to live within silos rather than on an operational farm. While a stated objective becomes our final destination, the relationships and decisions we make build the path upon which we will travel. How you lead (or relate to others) ultimately determines whom you lead.

- **_DELEGATE RESPONSIBILITY AND AUTHORITY TO THOSE AROUND YOU._** Good leaders analyze strengths when assigning projects to maximize the potential for successful resolution – they recognize what others can (and cannot) do, then work within those parameters to optimize the chances of success. If an individual has the ability to perform a task and is not overloaded with interfering assignments, much will be accomplished IF the leader avoids micro-managing activities (while remaining available for questions). Individuals must have the desire to contribute – must feel empowered to identify alternative actions and enabled to act independently – before they will risk failure (or taste success).

- ***ACCEPT THAT FAILURE IS AN EXCELLENT TEACHING TOOL.*** Far too many leaders feel that "winning at any cost" is the only way to be successful. While winning more often than not is desirable, if an individual never makes a mistake he or she will not know how to deal with adversity. Repeated failure should never be tolerated but if an individual can learn from a mistake – which is not dangerous, destructive or damaging to the organizations reputation or ability to perform – embrace the shortcoming and move beyond it (rather than dwelling within it).

- ***DEAL WITH ISSUES PROMPTLY AND APPROPRIATELY.*** If something needs correcting and discipline is required, administer it specifically and immediately. If an individual does something exceptionally well, celebrate as soon as possible. It is important to stop (or clone) the behavior rather than avoiding or ignoring it. One will not create mutually beneficial relationships if "everything is always wrong" and "nothing is ever right" in the actions, attitudes or behaviors of others. Focus on modifying the behavior to achieve different results rather than addressing the individual and expecting personality change.

Good leaders publicly celebrate success loudly while privately whispering (specifically and directly) about failure. They analyze themselves to identify their strengths (which they leverage towards a common good) and their weaknesses (which they work hard to strengthen OR minimize by leveraging another's gifts). A good leader may or may not be "a friend," but must ALWAYS be seen as fair and consistent. We must establish decision-making skills that allow us to act in a predictable and reasonable manner if we wish to become effective – which, if done by example rather than through edict – will allow us to accomplish great things with others.

ADDRESS INAPPROPRIATE BEHAVIOR

Some people seem to possess positive characteristics so distinguishing them from others that they seem to "walk on water." Others seem never to make mistakes – everything they touch turning to gold – their very presence tending to lift those around them to achieve better results. (While they truly ARE NOT always right nor do they ALWAYS make the right decision, they usually identify their errors and correct them quickly – before others can see negative results – rather than proclaiming them from the rooftops and revealing their woes for the world to see.) We see them as "super stars" shining brightly above all others – and they often see themselves as being above the crowd and beyond the fray. These rare individuals do not need much guidance – they simply need clear objectives and general direction from someone willing to get out of their way as they move forward to accomplish great things.

Increasingly (and unfortunately), it seems that people often seek success at the expense of others or wish to secure the "gains" of winning through the failures of others. These individuals do not look to see who may have been stepped on during their rise to the top nor what rules might have been broken (or at least bent badly) along the way. Whenever we find ourselves facing the reality of another's inappropriate behavior (whether it affects us personally or not) we should first identify how our actions (either explicit or implicit) may have condoned the behavior and what might we be able to do to alter that validation. We should look inward before striking outward – did something YOU said or expectations you imposed upon another drive him or her into an area outside of his or her core competency, experience or abilities – but MUST NOT excuse the results by giving a pass on the behavior. When helping an individual correct his or her inappropriate behavior we should establish how much of the blame we might realistically assume BUT must not build the net of deflection so strongly that responsibility is shifted away from the individual and onto his or her surroundings, experiences or the actions of others so none of the blame is assumed by the "offending party."

Discussing inappropriate behavior with another is naturally confrontational and never easy. In preparation, plan a course of action and a general direction that discussion might follow BUT do not "script" your conversation to the point that you end up "reading without leading" or talking rather than communicating. In their haste to avoid confrontation, many assume all the blame for other's poor behavior by praising their fulfillment of responsibility without passing on (or addressing) any of the actions taken to accomplish that what was done. Make sure you have fully communicated your expectations, are willing to acknowledge your part (if any) in the inappropriate actions, then act swiftly in addressing (and changing) them so they do not continue to reoccur. We can NEVER change behavior if we fail to address it, continue to ignore it or simply accept it as is because we would prefer to take the path of least resistance.

People do not really change much – they tend to be what they were allowed to become. Rather than trying to change people behaving badly we must identify (specifically) the inappropriate behavior causing the disruption then clearly and concisely communicate "why" that behavior must change – discussing the ramifications of continued poor behavior ALONG WITH the rewards of altered behavior. Only by focusing on the negative impact of continued inappropriate behavior – by defining an effect that can be linked directly to the cause - while detailing the rewards of appropriate behavior will inappropriate action ever be diminished (though, due to our human nature, it will never be totally addressed!). Ultimately, as with any change, we must make sure that the rewards of change are greater than the benefits of remaining the same – that more pain is experienced should one NOT change than might be experienced should they alter their path.

We will never address inappropriate behavior as long as we accept it (why would someone change without a compelling reason or reward)? Perhaps Pogo had it right when he said "We have found the enemy and it is us…" Unless (and until) we refuse to accept inappropriate behavior, we have only ourselves to blame for its existence!

THE SECRET OF MAKING GOOD DECISIONS

Many of the decisions we face will be made based on "what feels right" rather than a well thought out "cause/effect" response to a defined set of facts – a definitive "cookbook" recipe of right and wrong. Good decision makers see a high percentage of their "judgment calls" result in successful outcomes – often because they listen to the facts available, make a decision ONLY AFTER considering not only what could go wrong but also what could go right, and anticipate alternative directions and responses prior to their becoming necessary. People who fail to thoroughly think through the potential results of their actions BEFORE initiating them often create more negative or "questionable" results than they do positive and should probably avoid roles where making sound decisions is an essential part of their daily routine.

Good judgment is the basis of all positive outcomes when making decisions and is truly an experience-based characteristic. In order to make more "good judgments" than bad we must actively seek a variety of experiences upon which we can draw to make good choices – we must learn from failure or we will fail to learn. Rarely can we assume a position of authority without having first experienced many different roles and responsibilities that allow us to win and to recover from our losses. Visualizing how one situation applies to another – dealing with the practical application of situations rather than just the theoretical facts – is a transition that many find difficult. (Probably the TWO exceptions to this rule are being in a personal relationship or being a parent. No experience or prior knowledge is typically available and there are no "proven methods guaranteed to work." Reading a book will give you one person's perspective. Reading many books will provide multiple perspectives. LIVING THROUGH the situation is the only way to gain your own perspective! Perhaps that is why so many people feel at a loss when sharing a relationship or raising children!)

Good choices are more often the result of many small decisions – seeing and reacting to how they impact each other on the road to a major decision – than the infamous "ah-ha" moment creative and innovative trainers attempt to reveal. Great decisions are the result of careful analysis, thorough investigation, and a conscious, willful implementation of an action plan intended to initiate cautious forward movement. We never have all the answers – nor should we assume we have even asked all the right questions – but when we choose to move it MUST be with a sense of confidence that inspires others to follow.

We must continually expose others within our sphere of influence to new and different situations as we apply our knowledge – allowing them to grow by failing and feeling safe in doing so – if want them to develop their own breadth of experiences from which future decisions can be made independently from our own. Until another is developed and ready to carry on for us we cannot ascend the "ladder of success" as we will never make it past the first rung. When we make ourselves irreplaceably valuable at responding to and putting out fires we find our skills and talents cannot be "spared" to do anything else. The best "doer" in the world often fails as a leader because he or she fails to release what they did well when trying to assume new responsibilities – serving two masters rather than mastering one.

Making good decisions is part of a process rather than an event. As situations change, so should our willingness to shift direction. Once decisions are made we should move on to other challenges rather than dwelling on the action taken and agonizing on those not taken. Time does not stand still nor rest on its laurels - Do YOU?

INTROVERTED MANAGEMENT

Some would suggest that one must be an extrovert to be a good manager – that one must be heard (clearly and frequently) to be followed. We often think that highly effective managers must be able to speak flawlessly (and persuasively) to crowds or mingle effortlessly at events with public officials and other executives. Extroverts having KNOWLEDGE, EXPERIENCE AND ABILITY are able to mobilize individuals to follow them when they step into the spotlight but introverts often become excellent (and highly respected) leaders if they can overcome the tendency to hide (or downplay) their strengths.

During my 25 years of promoting operational excellence and business sustainability through the efforts of The Employers' Association, I have met a number of successful leaders who are successful, universally admired and respected. Many of the better leaders have been more "introverted" than "extroverted" in their actions, communications and ways they influence those around them. Though extroverts can often motivate individuals with ease and inspire them to do things they might not have otherwise considered, some extremely introverted individuals have become excellent leaders when they exhibit basic characteristics not typically associated with extroverts. These tendencies would include:

- Introverts are often deliberate and measured in their responses to situations. This does not mean they are slow (many process things quickly) but rather that they have considered the "pros and cons" of most decisions and formulated several alternative courses of action should their initial direction prove untenable. They are not prone to bursts of temper or extreme reactions as they are more thoughtful in how they sift through and process information – rarely acting until they know (or have considered) what might happen should they act. Introverts respond strategically to most situations rather than emotionally – establishing trust and confidence in those that choose to follow their lead.

- Introverts are analytical in their thought processes – experts at finding their way through reams of data quickly and reaching the core of the matter. Subdued in words and actions (allowing more time to be spent "thinking" than "acting"), introverts are surprisingly decisive – any perceived delays in action being caused by an introvert's need to view issues from all sides rather than their fear of acting to resolve issues.

- Introverted leaders are good listeners. Being naturally quiet, they let others do most of the talking BUT listen closely to everything said around them. Being deliberate and intentional in their actions, introverts act on what they hear after filtering "what will work" from "what will not" so their decisions are likely to be accepted by "the team" rather than rejected as being a "top-down" proclamation.

- Introverts are naturally risk averse – a critical management function in avoiding potentially disastrous risk. While new ideas, products or services must be considered when charting an organization's future, the ramifications of intentionally changing a product, process or service must be anticipated (and alternative directions be developed) should "our worst nightmare" come true. Being "risk averse" helps to minimize nightmares but to remain "as we are" insures nothing but certain death. While we must change to grow, we must take risk wisely when others depend on the decisions we make (or choose not to make).

- Introverted leaders often become the voice of reason within any situation or environment. While an introvert's voice is not typically loudest, it often becomes the one to which most listen. Influenced more by rationality than charisma, an introverted leader is "heard" because people know something reasonable is being said in a rational and thoughtful way.

To be successful as an introvert in management, you have to be willing to force yourself out of your comfort zone. (I can speak from experience on this factor. A Board member once told me I would have to become more involved in the community if I were to lead this organization. Having served on more than twenty Boards and/or committees – typically 12 to 15 at any given time – I thank (or blame) this Director for his wisdom!) An introverted leader must be willing to make him- or herself get up and speak in front of people, run large and contentious meetings, and wade into interpersonal conflict when their natural inclination might be to go home and read a good book or be "an island" rather than a part of a larger society.

While extroverted individuals are often thought to be the best leaders (perhaps because they proclaim themselves as such), many qualities that make people more "introverted" are exhibited by great leaders. Listening before acting, analyzing before deciding and determining direction on the magnitude of risk (rather than the aversion of it) are characteristics of an introvert – AND of a great leader. Perhaps at no time in history has it been truer than today that we can become anything that we would like – regardless of our natural tendencies or reactions to things – as long as we take intentional action and "own" our failures (as well as our successes) while we act to decide by deciding to act.

PATHWAYS AND PASSAGES THROUGH LIFE...

A collection of lessons dedicated to those willing to dream the impossible while seeking the improbable...

    To those willing to reach for the stars when establishing their reality...

        To those who would accept what could be as a destination rather than being content with what is...

    To those willing to innovate as they fulfill their dreams...

To those accepting the responsibilities of LIFE within a world that too often rewards the status quo.

LIFE GOES SOFTLY

Life is a gift – but we often feel we should be able to hold it in our own hands, unwrap whenever we want and play selfishly with it so that we might find gain when others feel pain. Anyone can steer a ship through a calm sea – it takes a master to find safety within a storm. We must learn that life provides us with a plethora of opportunities and a fistful of challenges – that there are some things we can control and others that will only frustrate us should we resolve to understand them. We tend to compartmentalize and restrict ourselves when we focus upon how many breaths we are given in life – opening up our horizons to a world of possibilities only when we seek moments that take our breath away.

I have been exposed to both happiness and grief recently – both the beauty of the Creator and the loss that accompanies His creation's departure. I have seen incomparable power in the mountains, rivers and streams He created and experienced the hollow feelings that one's unexpected death left behind. I was brought to the heights of this world when a loved one's sickness was overcome yet brought to my knees when one far too young was taken away. As humans, we have an issue of control – wanting to control all things that touch our lives so that we can have what we want when we want it. As a point of reality, we must recognize those things we can control, those things that are out of our control, and seek the wisdom to know the difference.

The Breath of the Night…

He came lightly upon the breath of the night…
Dancing with reckless abandon across the meadows of their minds…
Flying carelessly through the shadows of their souls…
Seeking only to bring joy to those who would know him…
Sharing himself freely with any who might care.

He came lightly upon the breath of the night…
Lighting but for a moment before moving on…
Touching down but long enough to hint of his presence…
Leaving those who missed him searching for meaning…
And those he touched during his brief stay wanting for more.

He came lightly upon the breath of the night…
Blending with the quiet whispers of the ocean…
Warming the cool, damp evening air…
Bringing the light of day to an oppressive existence…
Opening the eyes of those too blind to otherwise see.

He came lightly upon the breath of the night…
Dreams of his laughter filling the now silent air with music…
Thoughts of his smile making the brightest of stars seem pale…
His brief reality lifting the veil from a world of sorrow…
Shining brightly within a troubled night trying to hide dread within its darkness.

He came lightly upon the breath of the night…
His brightness a contrast to the world's muted shades of grey…
His presence a member within the hearts of all who would have known him…
Forever changing a world into which he chose to only briefly enter…
Now looking down upon us cradled safely within the arms of God.

He left as suddenly as he came…
Not given the time to accomplish all he had intended…
Not fulfilling the promise of his physical being…
Not touching the lives that may have thrived in his presence…
Leaving lightly upon the breath of the night.

Perhaps we could find purpose in each passing – find joy in each moment – rather than holding on so tightly to our losses that we are stifled and destroyed. Perhaps we should embrace the fact that we cannot control everything nor ever know the reasons that things happen. Perhaps it is better to ask the right questions – those that help us find meaning within (and because of) each moment – so that we can eventually move forward towards the hope and promise of a brighter tomorrow as we, too, drift lightly upon the breath of the night.

YOU ARE DEFINED BY WHAT YOU DO - NOT WHAT YOU SAY

Perhaps it is just human nature that when the "going gets tough" most of us start blaming someone else. It is rare that, during the heat of an argument, someone will stop the conversation to take responsibility for the misunderstanding by saying, "Don't worry about it – it was not your fault. I totally messed up and take the blame for the problems we're having." More often than not an argument is peppered with "It is your fault!" or "We never would have been in this position had it not been for you!"

Imagine living in a glass house – where everything we say or do is open for critique and criticism. Nothing is "secret" or "private" when it comes to the choices we make or the actions we take. Such is the reality of leadership – and the tremendous weight of responsibility placed upon a leader's shoulders by those looking up to him or her. Extending this "glass house" concept fully to management (whether it be managing a company, a department or providing leadership to a family), it is hard to convince others to NOT do something when they see you do similar things yourself. How can you expect your employees to adhere to an "eight to five" schedule if your own day frequently begins at eight fifteen or ends at four thirty? (Forget about the fact that you might have been doing company business the previous night, or that lunch was more of a thought than an action, or that breaks are not part of the daily routine…people SEE you coming in late, or leaving early, and expect that to apply to them, too.) Parents tell their children to obey the rules (as they break the speed limit driving them somewhere), to listen to their teachers (as they complain about the "boss that does not know anything"), and to take time to enjoy life (when they are "too busy doing their own thing" to play catch in the yard). Far too many manage by edict rather than by example – a technique that might produce temporary results but cannot possibly create loyalty, respect or independent decision-making skills. We cannot be perfect, but some rules I would suggest for managing life (by living in a glass house) would include:

- ***Recognize that your actions speak far more loudly than do your words.*** Some may hear what we say but EVERYONE sees what we do. As a child I was taught that "seeing is believing." Never was I told that "hearing makes things right." Whether you deal with people as a manager, a peer, a friend, or as part of a family, those around you establish their perception of you by what you do…by how you act…not by the things you say about yourself. To be viewed as credible you must ACT credibly.

- ***Look for the good in others, loudly praising their positive actions and interactions while quietly addressing their shortcomings.*** People usually see what others do wrong…rarely recognizing or acknowledging what they do right. As I go through the store I rarely hear a parent saying, "You are really being a good shopper today!" to their child. Rather it's "don't touch," "wait until we get home," and "I am never going to bring you shopping again!" Though we need to address negative behavior to correct it, we should also make an effort to acknowledge and verbalize appreciation for things done well. The next time you are involved in a heated debate with someone you care about, rather than saying "This is all your fault!" try to assume some of the responsibility yourself. People tend to react better when they know not only what they should not do (or have done) but also what they did (or are about to do) well!

- *Never throw bricks when you live in a glass house.* Though you may open the window before tossing your criticism out at a friend or co-worker, they rarely take the time to open the door before returning fire. When we view life as if we were living in a glass house – fully exposed to those around us with no place to hide our own errors and secrets – we find ourselves more understanding not only of what others do but also of the REASONS they do things. We are less apt to see fault in them when we first examine ourselves to make sure that we are without fault.

- Judge yourself using the same standards you apply to others. The greatest leaders of our times would never ask others to do what they would not do themselves. Truly great generals led their troops into battle rather than following them from behind. Parents must "walk the talk" if they want their children to learn. Managers cannot expect loyalty, efficiency and a good utilization of time from their employees even if they never demonstrate it themselves. Those in a relationship must treat their "mate" as they wish to be treated.

When we live as though we are in a glass house – without shades or coverings to hide what we are – we begin to concentrate on what we should be doing rather than focusing on what others should not be doing. When our actions speak louder than our words – when they begin to reinforce the things we intentionally set out to do – others will follow our example rather than our edict. They will seek our approval rather than seeking to escape our criticism. They will absorb our praise and grow towards the light rather than being sheltered from reality out of fear of failure.

We all live in a glass house of some kind – our thoughts, actions and attitudes on public display for the world to see. Perhaps we should take the time to wash the windows in our glass homes – it might help as much light shine in as we wish to shed on those around us!

SELF-EVIDENT TRUTHS

The dictionary tells us that an axiom is "A self-evident or universally recognized truth; an established rule, principle, or law; a self-evident principle or one that is accepted as true without proof as the basis for argument." We encounter "self-evident truths" everyday but tend to hold onto some more than others. Several that have captivated my imagination (as they guide my life) would include:

"INDIVIDUALS UNABLE TO SPEAK POSITIVELY ABOUT WHAT THEY DO ALWAYS RESORT TO SPEAKING NEGATIVELY ABOUT WHAT ANOTHER DOES." Far too many individuals find it easier to bring someone down to their level than to bring themselves to a higher plain. We cast stones without thinking that our own glass house could be easily shattered. We console ourselves by justifying that "everyone else does it" so it should be OK (even when we know what we are considering is wrong). Though elevating yourself is often far more difficult than pulling others down, we gain far more by lifting ourselves up – bringing others with us – than we could ever achieve by immersing ourselves within a pool of mediocrity.

"IF YOU CANNOT BE KIND, AT LEAST HAVE THE DECENCY TO BE VAGUE." I think of a saying from the classic Disney tale, Bambi, when I read this one. As Thumper's father told him, "If you don't have something nice to say about someone, it is better to say nothing at all." It seems that our society revels in the "details of the fall." We do not seek answers to unfortunate situations so that we can avoid them ourselves – rather we seek all the sordid details so that we can validate our own standing as being better than that of those around us. We do not seek details so that we can help – rather we seek them so that we can embellish them as we talk to others. Perhaps we SHOULD try to help more as we hurt less – seek to provide a cushion upon which others might land rather than an open abyss into which they will fall.

"EVERYONE BRINGS JOY TO MY OFFICE, SOME WHEN THEY ENTER, OTHERS WHEN THEY LEAVE." OK, so this one is tongue in cheek – but so appropriate! How often has someone interrupted you during the middle of a thought – as you were just about to solidify an epiphany that would surely change the world forever? Sure, we need others to live life to its fullest, but we all have times when it seems that others might "do more good" talking to someone else than they do disrupting our thoughts! Enjoy the variety that people give the world around you – if everyone thought and acted as you do it would be a terribly boring (or an extremely predictable) world!

Several axioms I have used as guiding principles include these "self-evident truths" penned by Ayn Rand – all mirroring the thoughts sent to me by Don (but from a slightly different perspective):

"A creative man is motivated by the desire to achieve – not by the desire to beat others."

"The hardest thing to explain is the glaringly evident that everybody has decided not to see."

"Achieving life is not the equivalent of avoiding death."

One of my favorites (that I have not yet listed) is one of removing limitations we place in our own path: ***"The question is not who is going to let me – it is who is going to stop me?"*** Do not become your own worst enemy by becoming a roadblock – by believing a dream to be impossible, abandoning it before the journey towards its realization can even begin. Remember that all things are possible – some take a little longer to accomplish as they require more creativity, thought or planning – improbable does not equate to impossible!

ACHIEVING ONE'S POTENTIAL REQUIRES MORE THAN LUCK

Sometimes, because of a unique thought, appropriate timing, or plain good luck an individual is able to succeed, grow and prosper in spite of (rather than because of) the things he or she does. More often, however, much planning, analyzing, forecasting, modeling, and "sweat equity" go into making a venture successful. A successful individual must selflessly invest his or her time, money and effort to bring a dream to fruition. Before accomplishing anything, however, one must envision the desired future, determine what must be done (and how much one is willing to risk or sacrifice) to reach it, then steadfastly advance towards its realization. Along the way, progress must be monitored to identify obstacles that could hinder the accomplishment of goals AND to justify warranted changes to established plans. An individual will never reach his or her full potential should they focus too intently upon the path rather than the prize at its conclusion.

In order to grow, one must envision the future. What does one WANT to be, WANT to accomplish, can realistically EXPECT to achieve? One must start with a conclusion – a goal or set of expectations – if he or she is going to accomplish exceptional things. Without an end point, one will never know when one chapter has been concluded so that another can begin. Without "a beginning", one will never know when progress has been made or change has been initiated. Life without purpose can be eventful but is rarely satisfying. It may be full of new beginnings but is strangely at a loss for "ends."

Once a goal has been established, one must determine how it can be enacted. What knowledge or ability must be attained to achieve the goal? Who must be brought into the solution and who should be excluded from its execution? Must the power of a team be brought into play or is the goal more individualistic? Too often, training is an afterthought to the accomplishment of a dream. When we start "doing" without thinking we may taste limited success but it will be realized in spite of ourselves rather than because of anything that was intentionally done or could be repeated.

To achieve greatness, people MUST steadfastly advance towards the realization of their dreams (those without dreams rarely achieve greatness). In order to continually move forward, systems must be put in place to identify obstacles that could hinder progress AND to justify warranted changes. An individual will never reach their full potential should he or she focus too intently upon the path rather than moving towards the prize at its conclusion.

Throughout life we should take the time to "refresh our batteries"…to chart our own path…to set our targets high…so that we can be an integral part of a well-planned solution RATHER THAN simply a piece of the puzzle or part of the problem. Only by choosing to envision the future, to enact a solution and to steadfastly advance towards self-actualization (while keeping your eyes on the goal) will one achieve their true potential.

BUILDING AND MAINTAINING STRONG RELATIONS

One cannot do ONLY what is expected if one wishes to gain as much from a relationship as one contributes. Looking back (finding comfort in what once was rather than seeking it in what has not yet materialized), remaining content within the present (rather than using the present as a springboard to the future), and doing only what works (as opposed to seeking what might work better) are all signs of relationship stagnation. In order to assure that life-changing relationships are being developed and maintained, we should strive to:

- ***Clarify the difference between efficient and effective communication.*** An e-mail may be efficient, but a conversation could more effectively resolve an issue without extended "replies and clarifications." Effective employees make sure that every investment of time and/or energy has a direct and measurable impact on their organization's ability to conduct business. Effective relationships begin with a foundation of sharing – one of giving more than you would ever expect to take – resulting in more than you could ever dream possible.

- ***Avoid the misguided concept of being irreplaceable.*** No individual is irreplaceable. If an individual feels that nobody could EVER do what he or she does, that person has probably limited what he or she will ever be able to accomplish. Individuals who believe they are "critical" to another person OR an organization because of their limited and specialized role simply reinforce stagnation and the acceptance of the status quo.

- ***Quit believing you know all the answers.*** People who know to ask the right questions are much more valuable (and desirable) than those who try to give all the right answers. One must always be open to new ideas, techniques, and ways of doing things. We can truly contribute to a meaningful relationship ONLY after identifying the limitations of current processes, practices, systems and procedures by asking questions that identify and isolate deficiencies – then by taking intentional action in a manner that defines a new direction and establishes a better destination.

- ***ALWAYS give credit to others.*** Individuals who recognize and acknowledge the ideas and actions of others – rather than taking credit for thoughts that may not be their own – tend to rise more rapidly to the top and find more satisfaction in close relationships. When credit is freely given (with accountability being assigned and accepted should mistakes occur), people learn from their mistakes (rather than being flogged for them). Ultimately, the individual initiating the thoughts and the person allowing their development will jointly own the benefits of another's ideas allowed to grow and prosper.

A continuous source of water – of ideas – must be available if we wish a pond to become a lake – and an even greater source must exist if we seek to expand a lake into an ocean. For one to realize "what could be" rather than simply bringing to fruition "what is," a variety of ideas and abilities must be channeled into a single solution rather than being diverted into unrelated tributaries that flow uncontrolled away from the goal. It is only by giving without expectation that we will ever receive without limitation.

MAKE A DIFFERENCE THROUGH ALL YOU SAY AND DO

Everyone should "make a difference" in life – but what "making a difference" means is not the same to everyone. Some would think that making a difference means to change the world while others might think getting through the day by helping to provide the needs those depending upon them might have is the greatest difference they might make. Some might think they can make a difference by fulfilling their dreams – by bringing to fruition their boldest imaginings – while others might wish only to dream without being awakened by the nightmare of things outside their control. Some might wish for fame, fortune or other recognition – to be "that person" the world places upon the pedestal of success. Others might hope to survive the darkness that shrouds their day – to see a tomorrow brighter than today.

Making a difference is the foundation upon which we build self-confidence and values – the base from which we establish who we are and what we wish to become. Building upon a firm and solid foundation can help us make a lasting difference – allow us to carry a heavy load without losing stability or drifting aimlessly without purpose. Far too many people, however, prefer to build upon shifting sands and untested principles – seeking monumental results with minimal effort.

Some people dream of success – of being something or somewhere else – preferring to remain in the comfort of their sleep without investing the sweat equity or emotional capital needed to bring transformation. Others wake from their dreams and begin working to bring them to fruition – to put into action the thoughts that came to them while sleeping by taking intentional action to move them forward. Taking action – ANY action – provides us the opportunity to make a difference. When trying to make a difference, the only "wrong" decision is one not made – the only "inadequate" action is one not taken.

We can all make a difference in life – but not all of us will make the same difference. Some are working on becoming all they might become – having very little energy (or inclination) to make a difference in the life of another. They take one day at a time – living a life that seemingly offers more redundancy than reward, more sense of survival than source of stimulation. Others seem always to give back far more than they could ever receive – finding more joy in the journey than delight in the destination.

Making a difference is affecting the lives of those around you SO THAT your life might change. It is pulling others up with you rather than crawling over their backs as you reach for the top. It is adding value to the lives of others, knowing that doing so will make a difference in their own life. It is bringing a smile to the face of another – of sharing another's troubles so that you can join them in their joy.

To make a difference you must BE different. When you begin to THINK differently, you will find yourself floating to the top as those around you rise to the surface rather than trying to swim against the current while ascending on your own. You will embrace change rather than fearing failure – seeking the possible rather than accepting the probable. Make a difference in others – the return on your investment will make a difference in you!

CHANGE YOUR ATTITUDE TO MAKE A DIFFERENCE

Far too often we become disillusioned with what we have – seeking other rewards or greener pastures – without first identifying OUR OWN role in the disappointment we feel. People confronted with occupational crisis or personal catastrophe rarely ask themselves what they did (or did not do) to contribute to their situation. We tend to walk away from problems by blaming others rather than facing the reality that our own actions or decisions may be (or have caused) a major share of the problem. We turn our backs on relationships that have cooled rather than trying to feed the fire only to find that the smoldering embers we thought had died can often provide a much hotter flame when fanned than the roaring fire built and fed with kindling.

Some people seek something for nothing – asking not what they can do to contribute to the well-being of others but rather what others can do to elevate their own well-being. They expect others to provide for them – be it income, a job, an opportunity, comfort, warmth, security or a plethora of other things. They seek all that others have without working to possess it. They want all that others enjoy without saving or investing the sweat equity needed to earn it. They want all things possible handed to them without putting forth the effort needed to initiate change. Rather than lifting themselves up they seek to bring others down – to take what they feel they deserve from the efforts of others rather than contributing to what they receive through their own initiative. They seek change and acceptance from others when they have failed rather than trying to lift themselves up after acknowledging and owning their shortcoming. These people are part of the problem with this world rather than part of the solution – part of the illness we fight rather than part of the cure.

Some people seek to build upon "what is" as they pursue what is not yet theirs – often seeking to realize things or situations not yet fully imagined. They see life as opportunity rather than entitlement. They may fall two steps back with every step they take BUT never stop moving as they seek to accomplish their clearly established goals. These people accept responsibility for their actions should they contribute to failure, either learning from the mistake so that it will not be repeated or correcting the problem by addressing their individual shortcomings. They see a relationship as a living, breathing organism – something that needs to be nurtured through constant attention and feeding rather than allowed to drift aimlessly on its own without constant caring and sharing. They see our land of freedom and opportunity as a place where extreme individual efforts results in unprecedented reward – where nothing is outside the reach of those willing to work hard to bring possibilities to fruition. These people are part of the solution in life – part of what "could be" rather than rooted in "what is." They seek (and eventually achieve) what is possible rather than being content to live out the probability that life holds for those willing to wait for what may eventually come.

In order to MAKE a difference in life, you must be willing to BE different. You cannot remain "one of the crowd" doing things the same way they have always been done if you expect change. If you feel the world owes you something you do not currently receive you should look to see what effort you have invested to deserve the reward you seek. If you think others are receiving the rewards you deserve you should try to duplicate their investment or replicate their efforts so you, too, might generate a favorable return (rather than expecting it to be provided to you by another).

Your future lies firmly within your own control, but the picture it holds may be vastly different based on where you cast your vision. Those looking over their shoulder tend to live in the past – finding comfort in what was but never realizing what could be. Those seeing their present as all they could ever need or want will rest on their accomplishments without reaching out to grasp the attainable rewards that might not yet be available. Those casting their vision forward – seeing the potential of where they are going as being well worth the risks – accept the challenges an unknown future presents as opportunities rather than threats. To make a difference, dwell upon "what was" only long enough to recognize the value your past contributes to the decisions you must make and the actions you must intentionally take to bring your future to fruition. Reach up as you reach out – lifting others with you as you climb the ladder of success – and the difference you make will be felt through all of time.

<u>LIVING LIFE</u>

Some people go through life without making waves. They follow the crowd and minimize the attention that making independent decisions or entering uncharted waters might bring. They take highly travelled routes to well-known destinations, thereby avoiding unknown, unproven or untested territories. The compliant live a safe existence taking few risks while receiving occasional rewards. Seen by many as successful, these individuals act in a predictable manner to achieve accomplishments already reached and perfected by others. They are keepers of the status quo – willing to do whatever is required to maintain an existence offering much comfort with little risk. They establish a satisfactory and acceptable level of success while virtually eliminating the potential of failure. They rarely lose big within their sheltered existence – yet one might question how much can be gained if very little is risked. The world needs people willing and content to "do what is right and acceptable" as they fill defined roles and accomplish assigned tasks – but more than compliance is needed if we are to experience all that life might offer or fulfill the potential we all could realize.

I would prefer to associate with people willing to take risks – however calculated or intentional they may be – in order to accomplish new things and define new horizons. People who look at a sunrise as the beginning of an unknown adventure rather than the end of night's darkness are visionary leaders. People who see what could be rather than live within what is – or what has been – have unlimited potential. I seek those willing to say "no" to what is acceptable and understood as they travel paths not yet paved while seeking destinations not yet finalized. I prefer to associate with individuals who recognize the crowd as a reality but refuse to be a part of it (UNLESS they choose to lead it to a new horizon). They see the sky as a possibility rather than as a limit. Theirs is a world of "what if" rather than "what is." To these achievers, each new destination is but a resting place – a brief respite within a lifelong journey rather than a landing zone used to establish a permanent settlement. New beginnings are common to those seeking closure to what has been while seeking what might yet be. They are foreign to those finding comfort in what is – seeking shelter from the unknown within the well-defined.

Life is a choice between two paths – one leading towards the sky, the other leading towards the valley. We can take the road most travelled and find comfort within the valley – find a proven lifestyle providing rich and predictable rewards – OR we can seek the rarified atmosphere of the mountaintops – find a new horizon in whichever direction we wish to look. We all choose which path we wish to travel – neither path being totally "right" or completely "wrong." We live with our choices – hold fast to the possibilities (or the probabilities) that our actions dictate. Whether you are a seeker or a planter – a dreamer or a doer – if you invest all of yourself into your intentional actions you will receive back all that your choice allows – limited only by your own acceptance of (or refusal to accept) reality.

MOVING SAFELY FROM YOUR LILY PAD TO THE SHORE

Far too many people view their goal – the place they want to "land" or the person they wish to become – as their destination rather than as but a stop along the way. They view the end of their journey being more important than the path they take to arrive. We often travel as if wearing blinders that focus our view on where we are going once we leave where we are so that NOTHING will distract us from getting where we want to be. Life can teach us many lessons if we learn from our false starts and misdirection as we attempt to reach our goals.

Think of how many businesses have shut down because they were unwilling (or unable) to transform themselves into something other than what they were. When high performance eight cylinder engines were the norm rather than the exception – and when quality was hoped for rather than expected – companies were very successful making piston rings. As four cylinder engines became more prevalent – and quality became synonymous with extended use and high mileage – the market evaporated and many parts suppliers shut down because they could not re-purpose themselves. Family farms are being sold to corporate entities because they cannot compete now that refrigerated transportation has expanded the concept of "marketplace" from local to international. Small town grocery, hardware and department stores have become an oddity as large superstores and "big box retailers" have taken over the landscape. Businesses that thought they had arrived – that were content with where they were rather than looking towards where they might want to be – have become but memories. Unfortunately, people can find themselves in a similar situation should they choose contentment with what they are rather than reinventing themselves into what they could become.

Many people stall and delay – doing anything to keep from making a decision to change – until forced to move because what was once secure is gone. We wait far too long to realize that we live on a lily pad – an isolated resting spot within a large lake that will eventually wither and die. When our safe haven is threatened enough that we are finally pushed to leave, many may jump without thinking about where they might land. We tend to leap before we look – sometimes exchanging our temporary resting spot for a greater danger lurking beneath its surface. In our impatience, we jump upon the first train leaving the station without checking to see if another form of transportation might be more effective.

Rather than delaying or postponing our decisions until we are faced with disaster like the companies that could not transform themselves into something different, perhaps we should focus not only on where we wish to be but also on why we wish to relocate AND what might be the result of doing nothing. We should identify alternative approaches that might be more (or less) beneficial than the obvious leap into the water (potentially directly into the gaping mouth of a lurking predator!) before we jump towards a quick solution – yet also weigh the benefits of INTENTIONALLY doing nothing until we are sure what will result from our actions.

Whether we read a map, listen to a navigation device or look on-line for directions, when travelling we seek our destination but could not arrive without figuring out what roads to take. We must anticipate roadblocks or detours, possibly setting aside resources for tolls and unexpected delays along the way. Why do we treat life so much differently? Rather than planning for the journey, anticipating what might go wrong and preparing for potential detours along the way we tend to focus more on moving from where we are to where we want to be without thinking much about how we plan to bridge the gap between here and there.

It has been said we should lead, follow or get out of the way. Perhaps the most critical of these is the last – for if you are not part of the solution (by either leading the charge or participating in the process) then you are, perhaps, a significant part of the problem (when you fail to engage and obstruct the progress of others).

Be all that you can be by first identifying what you might wish to become then focusing upon the path you choose to take as you move forward. Look before you leap – then make sure you are ready, willing and able to learn from the journey as you reach out to accomplish your dreams.

David J. Smith, CAE – President & CEO of The Employers' Association

I look at business through a poet's eyes. Though writing is not my livelihood, it makes up a large part of my life. Having grown up in a small community in the Midwest, I spent hours in the woods…by lakes… near streams…sharing creation with a handful of close friends through the eyes of an innocent child. When others saw danger in storms, I saw awesome power. Where others sensed fear in being alone, I focused on the subtleties of life that present themselves only in the silence of solitude…on the motion of the wind, on the power of the sea as it pounded upon a seemingly secure shoreline, on the current of a stream as it swept away a child's dreams…on the depths of emotions…on living within a dream while reaching out towards an undetermined destiny.

I contribute to and edit The Employers' Association newsletter (***Executive Update***), publish a BLOG (***Dave's Deliberations***) and have written for both The Grand Rapids Business Journal (***People Matters***) and MiBiz (***The Human Factor***). While my poems have been published in several national anthologies, ***PATHWAYS AND PASSAGES TO LEADERSHIP*** is my first published collection. Should those who share my feelings on life, leadership, achievement, change and the realization of dreams embrace these writings, it will not be my last.

Sit back and ponder life as you read this volume…a collection of thoughts from the soul of a dreamer living within a business-oriented world. Study the "passages" in both word and picture as you make the transition from "doer" to "leader," or simply seek affirmation or confirmation of the position to which you have arrived.

Before we seek safe passage, we must first dream – for without dreams, we cannot achieve…

Before we determine which path we will follow, we must immerse ourselves in all things that could be possible rather than seeking only those things we can be sure of…

Printed in the United States
By Bookmasters